The Good Sam RV Coo

The Good Sam RV Cookbook

Edited by
Beverly Edwards and
the editors of Trailer Life

Trailer Lite Books
Agoura, California

Trailer Life Book Division

Richard Rouse
President

Ted Binder
Vice President/General Manager

Michael Schneider
Vice President/Publisher, Book Division

Rena Copperman
General Manager, Book Division

Cindy Lang
Assistant Manager, Book Division

Library of Congress Cataloging in Publication Data

The Good Sam RV cookbook.

   Includes index.
   1. Cookery. 2. Outdoor cookery. 3. Mobile
home living. I. Edwards, Beverly A., 1933—
II. Good Sam Club. III. Trailer Life.
TX840.M6G67   1987   641.5′752   87-6007
ISBN 0-934798-17-6

Cover illustration: Joyce Kitchell
Cover design: Bob Schroeder
Interior design: Bert Johnson, Graphics Two
Interior illustrations: Cliff Robertson
Managing editor: Rena Copperman
Editorial assistants: Judi Lazarus, Martha Weiler
Indexer: Rose Grant

10 9 8 7 6 5 4 3 2

This book was set in ITC Eras and Galliard by Publisher's Typography
and printed by Arcata Graphics at Kingsport, Tennessee.

To RV cooks everywhere;
may their spirit of adventure
always be with us.

Contents

Winners

Adamson, Margaret, Vegetable Pizza Salad, 60
Almond, Grace, Lemon Brownies, 190
Ansalvish, Charlotte L., Spaghetti Salad, 58
Beek, Carole, Lemon Squares, 191
Bentekovics, Ricardina, Trim and Slim Flank Steak, 124
Bond, Dorothy, Mama Mia Salad, 61
Bradshaw, Vieno M., Finnish Flatbread (Rieska), 81
Brand, Marjorie, Tropical Cream Pie, 201
Bristol, Dolores, Ladyfinger Cheesecake, 180
Brown, Mildred S., Bean Salad Supreme, 49
Campbell, Norma, Everlasting Salad, 51
Clark, Lillian, Jalapeño Jelly Camp-out Dip, 30
Clark, Loretta, Punch Bowl Cake, 186
Cole, Joan, Baked Broccoli with Cheese, 99
Collette, Peggy, Banana Cupcakes Supreme, 168
Cook, Elizabeth, "Stuff", 120
Cummings, Virginia S., Zippy Zucchini Casserole, 107
Cummins, Virginia, Chocolate Dream, 181
Daymude, Kathleen, Alaska Cheesecake, 179
Elrod, Phyllis, Peanut Butter Temptations, 192
Fairfield, George, Dynamite Fixin's, 116
Faller, Ethel L., Easy Spread Cake, 171
Felton, Marlene, RV Chicken Delight, 130
Fleagle, Dorothy M., Cookies in a Cup, 196
Geiger, Helen, Shipwreck, 118
Hallen, Lucille E., My Favorite Turkey Loaf, 126
Hamre, Ilene, Tangy Orange-Pinapple Cake, 171
Harmer, Frances, Pizza on a Bun, 134
Heryet, Betty, Lemon Bisque, 184
Horning, Lois, RV Skillet Chicken, 130
Howe, Gladys, Almond Delight, 189
Huett, Jean S., No-Bake Chocolate-Graham Torte, 186
Hunter, Betty R., Cheesecake Supreme, 177
Hyden, Lucy, Almond Float, 182
Jairell, Shirley, Happy Hour Special, 26
Jairell, Robert L., Caramel Corn Supreme, 206
Jennings, Dorothy, M., Pineapple Sour Cream Pie, 199
Jerard, Lynne H., Lynne's Sin, 188
Johnson, Bernice A., Sweet and Sour Meatballs, 121
Jones, Mae, Grated Sweet Potato Pudding, 187
Joos, Winifred J., Wild Rice and Shrimp, 142
Kellner, Madelene, Harvest Cake, 172
Kirlin, B. Fay, Savory Skillet Sausage, 138
Klinger, Catherine, Fast and Easy Mac, 119

Preface

For more than 20 years, TL Enterprises, Inc. and the Good Sam Club have been totally dedicated to the RV life-style. Since its inception, the Good Sam Club has been a means for those who own and use recreational vehicles to share their love of RVing and the outdoors with one another.

The growth of the Club led to the formation of chapters. Later, RV rallies, known as Samborees, brought members together for three days to a week of seminars and entertainment. Today, every state (except Hawaii) and six Canadian provinces have at least one Samboree every year, and the Club's International Headquarters sponsors other Samborees throughout the United States and Canada.

Born out of the wishes of a few RVers to aid one another on the road, the Good Sam Club has grown to encompass more than a half-million families. Over the years, these members have extended their abilities and desires to help others far beyond the RVing community.

Through individual members and more than 1,200 chapters, thousands of lives have been touched. Good Samers have raised over $200,000 to support Dogs for the Deaf, a program that provides hearing-ear dogs for people with impaired hearing. More recently, members have donated both time and financial assistance to Special Olympics, an international program that provides developmentally disabled athletes an opportunity to demonstrate their skills and improve self-esteem through athletic competition.

Other individuals and programs too numerous to mention have benefited from assistance provided by members of the Good Sam Club. From a motorist stranded on the highway to a child in need of a liver transplant, members of the Good Sam Club have been there to lend a helping hand, and a smile.

It is for them, and the spirit that they embody, that this book is written.

BEVERLY EDWARDS

Acknowledgments

To compile this cookbook has taken more than one year of cooperative effort on the part of members of the Good Sam Club, representatives of Trailer Life Enterprises, and many others without whom we could not have completed the project.

Special thanks go to the state and provincial directors who conducted cook-offs at their Samborees, and the hundreds of members who took part in these events as participants and judges. Their volunteer efforts are deeply appreciated.

We are grateful to Barbara Mona, home economist and teacher at Agoura High School, and the students in her coeducational advanced cooking class, Fall, 1986, for taking on the task of testing most of the recipes submitted by winners of state and provincial cook-offs. The students accepted the challenge as a class project, and met it head-on, providing us with valuable evaluation of the recipes.

Members of the Sagebrush Sams of Ridgecrest, California, planned a camp-out around a potluck comprised of additional recipes that required evaluation. Both cooks and tasters gave us needed information on the recipes they prepared.

Our final judges were Kristine Kidd, associate food editor at *Bon Appétit*; Hugh Carpenter, chef and authority on Chinese cuisine; and Ray Hughey, feature writer for the *News Chronicle,* Thousand Oaks.

This book would not have been possible without the many talents of Book Division Manager Rena Copperman. She was responsible for overseeing all aspects of the editorial and production stages from testing and judging to final printed copy.

Providing accurate and speedy production of type under the able direction of Mary King were Angela Pezzullo, Julie Vergel de Dios, and Project Manager Gale Urtel of Trailer Life's typesetting department.

Taking on the monumental task of editorial assistance were Judi Lazarus and Martha McCarty. Their diligence is appreciated.

A special thanks to Dometic Sales Corporation for the donation of three of their quality appliances as prizes.

Showing unending patience throughout the year was Sam Edwards, my husband.

Thank you one and all.

Introduction

Sharing is an important part of RVing the Good Sam way.

Good Samers have been known to share just about everything from a cup of sugar to an extra hose coupling. They share their time and their talents in helping one another, and they share their love of the outdoors. They also share their ideas.

It is this sharing of ideas that led to publication of our *Good Sam RV Cookbook*. It's no secret that Good Samers love to eat. Whether with another family or at a chapter potluck, they enjoy sharing their food and recipes with one another.

Through the Good Sam Club's first-time-ever cookbook, members can share their recipes and ideas not only with those they meet at camp-outs, but with the entire membership.

Good Samers also love contests. Drop in at any Samboree or chapter camp-out, and you'll see them ringing horseshoes, playing "jarts," or even tossing cowchips.

Because of this spirit of friendly competition, Trailer Life Books decided to select some of the recipes for this book through cook-offs held at Good Sam state and provincial Samborees. The directors were invited to organize these cook-offs at their 1986 Samborees. Twenty-six incorporated cook-offs into their Samboree schedules, selecting winners at each event. These state and provincial winners provided the nucleus for this cookbook.

Students in the coeducational advanced foods class at Agoura High School, located near Good Sam's International Headquarters, tested these state-winning recipes. Under the direction of instructor Barbara Mona, they accepted this challenge as a full-semester class project.

The Sagebrush Sams of Ridgecrest, California, assisted in testing, preparing a complete potluck dinner for their November camp-out using state-winning recipes.

With still a few recipes remaining to be tested, members of the Good Sam Club's Headquarters staff set aside their computers and typewriters and did their share of cooking. Those who did not prepare recipes did the tasting.

All of the judges for this testing procedure used the same tabulation form in determining eleven finalists. Points were given for availability and cost of ingredients, ease of preparation, color, aroma, texture, appearance, taste, ability to prepare ahead, presentation, ease of storage, nutritional value, and ability to be prepared in an RV galley.

The results of this year-long contest found Ricardina Bentekovics of Parsipanny, New Jersey, being named Good Sam Cook Number One for her *Trim and Slim Flank Steak* (page 124). Second place winner Dorothy Jennings of San Jose, California, won for her *Pineapple Sour Cream Pie* (page 199), and Della Wootan of Tucson, Arizona, took third place for her *Eggplant Parmigiana* (page 117). Each of these winners received a Dometic major kitchen appliance.

Runners-up included: Eileen Kuehl of Strawberry Point, Iowa, *Zesty Italian Meat Loaf* (page 123); Vieno Bradshaw, Poway, California, *Finnish Flatbread* (page 81); Joyce Wise, Chagrin Falls, Ohio, *Japanese Fruit Pie* (page 199); Elizabeth Cook, Greenwood, South Carolina, *"Stuff"* (page 120); Mary McConnell, Madison, Wisconsin, *Whisky Cake* (page 176); Phyllis York, Gorham, Maine, *Bakewell Cream Biscuits* (page 74); Marlene Felton, Victoria, British Columbia, *RV Chicken Delight* (page 130).

Once the field was narrowed to eleven finalists, students at Agoura High School once again prepared the recipes for judging. Judges for the final cook-off were Kristine Kidd, Hugh Carpenter, and Ray Hughey.

Although those who entered state Samboree cook-offs were eligible to compete for prizes, it wasn't necessary to enter a cook-off to be included in the cookbook. All Good Sam members were invited to submit recipes, using the official entry form. (Headquarters received more than 800 recipes!) From these, the cookbook staff selected recipes to supplement the cook-off winners.

In making final selections, the staff took into consideration a balance that covered all categories and provided recipes for nearly every occasion from small meals for two to potluck entrées.

Most of these recipes are designed for the traveling RV chef. Some can be prepared at home, leaving the weekend camper with more time to enjoy other activities. Others take advantage of nonperishable staples. Outdoor recipes are included, as are one-dish meals and delectable snacks. Many have time-saving hints accompanying them. Every recipe was created and submitted by a member of the Good Sam Club. We hope that you enjoy using this special cookbook as much as we have enjoyed compiling it. Happy RVing.

Winner Designation

Only those recipes submitted by the winners of the state and provincial cook-offs, and so designated in this book, have actually been tested for this publication. We also made a concerted effort to obtain the chapter affiliation of members whose recipes appear in this book, and to indicate all the winners (designated by a ribbon). If there were any omissions or errors, we apologize.

Time to Get Ready

The tulips are starting to bloom, and the open road is calling. Most of the snow has melted off the mountains, and thoughts turn to restocking the RV and heading for new adventures. For fulltimers and weekenders alike, having a well-stocked RV galley is essential for convenient cooking on the road.

The purpose of this chapter is to provide you with some ideas when setting out to the market to stock up for the road. Provisioning the RV galley is a lot like filling your pantry at home, except for one thing—think small. That large, economy-size box of cereal just won't fit in most RV galleys, where space is at a premium. The same goes for staples. Keeping a dozen cans of tomato sauce in your home pantry makes sense, but taking up that much space in an RV galley means having to cut down on something else.

Although every RV cook has different priorities about what to keep on board, the need for the basic staples is standard. And that's where those great stackable containers can be put to good use. If they are transparent, it's easy to see at a glance what's inside and when they need to be refilled from your home supply. Rectangular shapes leave no wasted space and stack better, too; before investing in a supply of these containers, measure the cabinet you plan to use and buy the appropriate sizes in order to conserve as much space as possible.

At the end of each RV outing, refill your RV canisters, and you'll be ready to roll out that much faster when next the lure of the open road calls. However, when it's time to put your rig in winter storage, it is best to remove all food products.

These handy containers come in a variety of sizes and are suitable for most staples, including everything from the usual (flour, sugar, pancake mix, and rice) to more individual items, such as popcorn and trail mix. Even dry cereals keep well in these containers.

Spices can be a real nuisance to store, but they are essential to tasty cooking. Some RVs have a built-in spice rack or space for one, but many rigs don't provide either a rack or a convenient place to put one.

One solution is to purchase small plastic bins. Spices and small items, such as those handy little seasoning envelopes, fit nicely into these baskets and are easily accessible. When preparing a recipe, keep the basket in a convenient place so seasonings are at hand when cooking. Storing spices inside a cabinet rather than on the countertop also keeps them cleaner. The small metal containers stack better than glass jars.

There are other space-savers on the market that make stocking the RV galley much easier than attempting to arrange it like your home kitchen. Three-tiered dish racks are great for those dead-end corners that nearly every RV seems to have in overhead cabinets. One- and two-tiered turntables also make the items toward the rear of the cabinet more accessible. Again, be sure to measure your space and pack items tightly, leaving little room for them to shift while the vehicle is moving. (You might consider some dividers.)

When shopping for dishes, keep in mind how and where they are to be stored. Those heavy plastic plates on today's market are beautiful, but they are heavy and take up a lot of space when stacked. If you're tired of plastic, you might consider some of those pretty new Corelle designs by Corning. This dinnerware is virtually unbreakable and stacks well.

The bulkiest items you'll be storing are pots and pans. If you're planning to treat yourself to some new cookware, measure the space where they're to be stored before making a major investment, or you might find you're an inch short of space to clear that drainpipe under the sink.

There also are other considerations when shopping for pans. Those decorated, enameled sets would look great on your stove, but they chip easily when stacked and subjected to movement and would need to be individually stored in padded bags to prevent marring.

The same goes for nonstick cookware; unless protected, the coating soon will wear off if the pans are nested. One way to avoid this is to layer towels between the pans; this also cuts down on rattling.

Paper towels are a necessity for the RV cook, and they are handiest if mounted on a wall rack well away from the stove. Unfortunately, some RV designers just haven't provided for a convenient place to put paper towels, and if the roll is placed on the galley counter, it usually gets saturated from spills. A handy solution is to purchase a vertical towel holder. It doesn't take up much space, and it keeps the towels from unrolling at an inopportune time.

The insides of cabinet doors provide additional space for smaller items. Shelves, hooks, and towel racks are available for almost every size door to hold spices, soap pads, brushes, measuring cups, and towels. Hooks mounted on the bottom of an upper shelf in the overhead keeps cups and mugs out of the way, too.

An especially handy door-mounted item is a small trashbag holder that contains a roll of these little bags. When one is filled and removed, another pulls up into place.

Overhead galley cabinets sometimes have space that could be better utilized by installing a second shelf. If this is to be done, measure the tallest item you will be storing on the lower shelf, and allow a one-inch clearance between that item and the upper shelf. If the upper shelf is only half as deep as the lower one, items in the rear of both will be more accessible. Be sure shelves have lips to keep items from sliding off when the vehicle is moving.

Even in the best-packed cupboards, bottles, dishes, and other items are going to shift toward the front of the cabinets as a result of parking and stopping the vehicle. To stabilize storage areas while moving, stuff pillows or towels in the cabinets to keep things in place. Lining utensil drawers with towels also will cut down on rattles.

Plan to store as few items on counter tops as possible. It's nice to have those little touches of home, but finding a place to put them when it's time to break camp is sometimes a challenge. If it is necessary to store odds and ends somewhere other than in a cabinet, line a sink with terry towels and put them in the basin when on the move.

Cooking in an RV galley can be fun, but having everything in a convenient place is essential.

What to Take Along (and Leave Behind)

Appliance stores are filled with tempting gadgets that do just about everything except read a recipe and assemble the ingredients. Even the kitchen in an average home wouldn't accommodate all of these wonderful inventions, and an RV galley is definitely not the place to accumulate them.

A few simple appliances should meet most needs. Everyone has different ideas as to what they consider essential (some can't get along without a toaster and others must have an electric skillet), but simplicity is the key word in deciding what to take along and what to leave behind. The following list is a guide; consider your personal needs when assembling your equipment.

1. Nearly every RV chef could use a small, hand-held electric mixer. They don't take up much more room than a conventional rotary beater and do a much better job of preparing a cake or whipping potatoes. Unless you park where there are electrical hookups every night, avoid purchasing a cordless electric mixer; you might not be hooked into shore power enough to keep the battery charged, and without it, the mixer won't work.

2. Many RVs come equipped with a built-in blender that can duplicate some of the functions of a food processor. If your RV is not so equipped, you might consider investing in one of the newer small food processors, especially if your usual menus call for much chopping and slicing. If not, the space could be better utilized for other items. Whatever you do, leave your large mixer at home.

3. For coffee drinkers, consider a space-saving, under-the-counter unit. They're out of the way and take up less space than a tea kettle to heat water for instant coffee.

4. A standard set of pots and pans will take care of most cooking needs. These usually include a 1-quart saucepan, a 2-quart saucepan, a 5-quart kettle, and a 10-inch skillet, all with lids.

   • A removable basket steamer in one of the pans is a bonus because the basket can double as a colander and stores neatly inside the pan when not in use. Keeping one extra small skillet on hand might be a good idea for sautéing onions while other pans are in use.

- The large kettle serves many purposes. It's good for a pot of soup, corn on the cob, or even for popping popcorn.

5. If you have sufficient storage space and like to cook shellfish, there's nothing like a crab cooker, or stockpot, but the need should warrant the space it occupies.

6. For baking pans, consider two standard sizes: $9 \times 13 \times 2$ inches and a 9-inch round cake pan. If you bake layer cakes, you might need two of the round pans, but only if you can fit two of them in your oven at the same time.

- In addition, a pie pan comes in handy for many uses other than baking pies, such as heating up leftovers.
- A jelly roll pan can be used for a cookie sheet or for catching drips when baking something on the upper shelf. Put a pretty kitchen towel on the pan and it becomes a tray for serving.
- For those who like angelfood or bundt cakes, a tube or bundt pan can do double duty—it also can be used as a salad mold.
- When buying baking pans, be sure you measure your oven before shopping. Otherwise you might end up with a jelly roll pan that's just a bit too long to fit in your oven.
- You also might want to keep some foil throwaway baking pans on hand for potluck suppers and for cooking extra-messy foods. They make cleanup much easier, especially when dry camped and on a limited water supply.

7. Make as many items as possible do double duty. A large measuring cup can serve as a mixing bowl, and soup bowls make perfect serving bowls for small meals. Juice containers can be put to work storing leftovers when not in use for juice. Mixing bowls with plastic lids are good for both mixing or storing food.

8. For hand utensils, a few simple items will handle most cooking chores. Start with a couple of large cooking spoons (one slotted), a cooking and barbecue fork, a short-handled spatula for indoor cooking, and a long-handled one for the barbecue, tongs (both long and short), and a set of sharp knives. For safety, it is imperative that knives be properly stored. Reaching into a drawer with a loose knife can lead to a serious injury. Knives should fit securely in holders. The knives that

come in self-sharpening sheaths are especially desirable because they will not accidentally fall out of the holders.

9. Linens need to be plentiful enough to keep a fresh supply between trips to the laundromat. Colorful linen towels purchased at tourist sites along the road make pretty and practical souvenirs when hanging in your galley. Add a pair of gloves and some pot holders to protect the countertops from hot foods, a sponge with a scrubber on one side, and a couple of dishcloths to your supply.

10. Containers to store leftover foods are essential. Margarine containers with secure lids work just as well as higher priced plastic bowls. They're lightweight, stackable, and come in a variety of sizes and shapes. Another handy container is an empty frozen juice can. It's a convenient place to pour hot grease or oil because it won't deteriorate and can be stored in the refrigerator.

RV galleys don't need to be large and elaborate to be useful. Getting away from our home kitchens reminds us that the simple life is a good life. Maybe that's what attracts so many people to RVing.

The Galley Refrigerator

One of the greatest advances in RV travel was the development of a refrigerator capable of operating on propane, a 12-volt battery, or conventional 110-volt electricity. The ability to keep food cold without depending on ice or shore (110-volt) power was a giant step forward in providing the RV cook with the convenience of a home kitchen.

Most of today's RVs are equipped with three-way refrigerators. The strides made by major RV refrigerator manufacturers have led to units that, for the most part, are equal to home refrigerators when it comes to cooling and freezing food.

However, the method used for cooling an RV refrigerator is somewhat different from the motor-driven compressor that cools a home refrigerator. While the RV refrigerator can be as effective in cooling and freezing food as a home-type unit, the following guidelines will insure better service:

1. Because of the need for the air to circulate (remember, it is necessary for the warm air to be removed), the manner in which food is stored in the RV refrigerator is important. The temptation to utilize every square inch of space will reduce cooling efficiency. It is essential that air be allowed to freely circulate throughout the food storage area; arrange the contents with this in mind.

2. It also is advisable to avoid large containers that cover a substantial area of shelf space and to avoid placing plastic liners on shelves, limiting circulation.

3. Moisture causes frost to form on the freezing compartment. To help prevent loss of moisture from beverages or food items stored in the refrigerator, make certain that anything containing moisture is well covered or sealed.

4. When preparing to use your RV refrigerator, allow ample time for the interior to cool down, preferably overnight. Starting a refrigerator with food already placed inside will greatly increase cool-down time. If it becomes necessary to cool the unit in a limited time, place a wrapped block of ice

or covered container of ice cubes in the unit, keeping the ice sealed for a minimum amount of evaporation.

5. When stocking the RV refrigerator for a trip, chill all items in the house refrigerator before transferring them to the RV refrigerator so the box can maintain a stable temperature after being stocked.

6. Opening a refrigerator door allows cool air to escape very rapidly. Try to avoid keeping the door open any longer than necessary. After a visit to the grocery store, unpack and place all items to be refrigerated near the unit before opening the door. Then place the food in the refrigerator as quickly as possible, opening the door only once.

7. If children are on board, you might want to consider keeping an ice chest in the RV for soda pop and snacks. Not only does this eliminate a lot of trips to the refrigerator, but it leaves more space in the unit for air circulation.

8. RV refrigerators are susceptible to changes in the ambient temperature, and thermostats need to be adjusted to coincide with these changes. In cold weather, setting the thermostat too low may lead to freezing in the cold storage compartment. In extremely hot weather, maximum cooling capacity probably will be necessary. It might be wise to invest in a refrigerator thermometer to monitor the temperature inside the refrigerator.

9. When selecting a campsite, there are two things to consider. One is to be sure the vehicle can be properly leveled, since an RV refrigerator must be kept level in order to function properly. It also is necessary to be sure that the exterior vent not be obstructed by parking too close to a building or another RV that might block proper air circulation on the exterior of the vehicle. In extremely hot weather, you might find it beneficial to prop open the exterior vent for better air circulation.

RV refrigerators are complex appliances, but if properly maintained should provide excellent service.

High-Altitude Cooking

If your RV travels find you camping in the Rocky Mountains, you probably will discover that your usual cooking techniques aren't producing the results you anticipate. Stovetop items take longer to cook, and baked items can produce disastrous results.

The lower atmospheric pressures at higher altitudes have a direct effect on food preparation. Water and other liquids boil at a lower temperature, and leavening in bread products has greater expansion during the cooking process.

By following a few simple guidelines, high-altitude cooking can produce properly cooked food.

1. It doesn't take long to realize that food does not cook as rapidly in high altitude. Just remember that the boiling point is at a lower temperature, and when cooking at a lower temperature, it is necessary to increase cooking time in order to get the results you expect.
2. Baking is a more delicate problem. Merely extending the time the food is exposed to heat will not solve the problem. The reaction time of leavening agents in high altitude is shortened, resulting in a product that is not properly cooked.
3. Flour also reacts to high and dry mountain atmosphere by becoming drier and absorbing more of the liquid ingredients in a recipe. To counter this, it becomes necessary to either reduce the amount of flour or increase the amount of liquid called for in a recipe. Cakes and breads not adjusted for high altitude will rise excessively, stretching and even breaking the cell structures, causing them to fall.
4. Sugar is another ingredient that sometimes must be slightly reduced in a recipe. The evaporation of liquid in a batter creates an excessive concentration of sugar that weakens the cell structure and also contributes to a fallen cake.
5. If using a cake mix, always look for and follow the high-altitude instructions.
6. Cookies are not as susceptible to high altitudes, but for better results, try decreasing baking powder or soda, fat content,

and sugar slightly, and increasing liquid ingredients and flour slightly. For pie crust, a little increase in a liquid ingredient might improve results.

Adjustments in baked goods need not be much to make a difference, and because of the variety of ingredients found in each recipe, it is impossible to provide a guide that will insure the desired results without restructuring the recipe. However, the following table should help individuals experimenting with high-altitude cooking:

Adjustment	3,000 ft.	5,000 ft.	7,000 ft.
Reduce baking powder; for each tsp. decrease	⅛ tsp.	⅛–¼ tsp.	¼ tsp.
Reduce sugar; for each cup, decrease	0–1 tbsp.	0–2 tbsp.	1–3 tbsp.
Increase liquid; for each cup, add	1–2 tbsp.	2–4 tbsp.	3–4 tbsp.

If you plan to spend a lot of time RVing at high altitudes and are having problems with your favorite recipe, contact a home economist at a Department of Agriculture extension office. He or she will guide you in adjusting for the altitude. It can be discouraging to take a cake out of the oven and watch it fall.

Next time you feel an urge to head for the hills, read up on high-altitude cooking and continue to enjoy all of your favorite recipes while parked on top of the world.

Appetizers, Dips, and Beverages

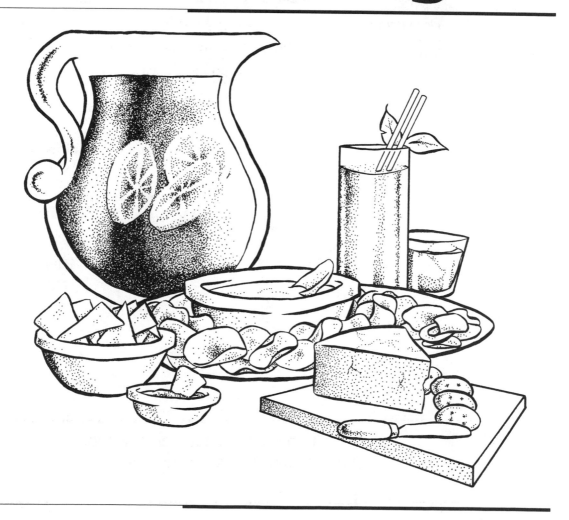

Cold Appetizers

William Purkett
Havre, Montana
Milk River Sams

One holiday season, when Bill's family was busy preparing Christmas food, he came up with this recipe. Tabasco sauce is the key ingredient, he tells us, and its festive look is great for holidays. Since it keeps well, it is perfect for parties, buffets, potlucks, and camp-outs.

Serves 30

Bill's Tangy Cheese Ball

2 8-ounce packages cream cheese, room temperature
2 tablespoons dried green pepper flakes
½ cup sliced green olives with pimientos
½ cup diced black olives
1 tablespoon instant dried minced onions
2 teaspoons Tabasco sauce
½ cup dried parsley flakes

Blend cream cheese, green pepper flakes, olives, onion, and Tabasco sauce with a fork in a medium-size bowl. Shape mixture into a round ball. Roll in parsley flakes until covered slightly, pressing flakes against ball as you roll it. Cover with plastic wrap and refrigerate for at least 1 hour before serving. Present on platter surrounded with snack crackers.

Hint: This will keep in the refrigerator for up to 2 weeks. You can add fresh sprigs of parsley around base of ball for an added festive touch.

It isn't so much what's on the table that matters, as what's on the chairs.

W. S. Gilbert

Death Valley Artichokes

LouAnn Hand
Exeter, California
Member at Large

Last year, when LouAnn and her family traveled to Death Valley, she took some artichokes along. Her recipe was such a hit with her group that she named the dish for the area.

Serves 4 or more

2 to 4 artichokes, outer leaves removed and cut in halves
1 lemon, quartered
1 8-ounce jar ranch-style dressing

Place enough water in heavy steamer to just reach bottom of steamer basket. Add lemon to water. Place artichokes in steamer basket, bring to boil, covered, and steam about 20 to 25 minutes, or until tender. Drain and refrigerate until serving time.

To serve, separate leaves from artichoke, remove fuzzy choke, and place on platter with dressing for dipping. (You'll have to toss a coin for the delicious prize—the bottom or fond.)

Dilled Onion Rings

Katherine Mellor
Vancouver, Washington
Cascade Sams

Katherine assures us that even people who cannot eat raw onions will be able to eat these tangy-flavored ones.

Serves 8 to 10

¾ cup sugar
¾ cup white vinegar
⅓ cup water
1 teaspoon salt
3 to 4 medium onions, thinly sliced
¾ teaspoon dry dillweed

Place sugar, vinegar, water, and salt in saucepan and bring to boil. Pour over sliced onions and dillweed that have been placed in a clean quart jar. Cover and shake several times as mixture cools to distribute dill. Store in refrigerator.

Hint: Katherine slices her onions directly into the quart jar.

Ethel Schenck
Helena, Montana
Treasure State Wheelers

If called on to provide appetizers for a crowd, try Ethel's liverwurst spread. It's easier to prepare when you have electricity (for the blender), so if you're going to be dry camped, make it before you leave for your camp-out.

Serves 60

Liverwurst Spread

1¼-ounces unflavored gelatin (1 envelope plus ½ teaspoon)
¼ cup cold water
1½ teaspoons beef bouillon granules
1½ cups hot water
1 3-ounce package cream cheese, softened
1½ cups (12 ounces) liver sausage
½ cup mayonnaise
2 tablespoons finely chopped green onions
Dash each of Tabasco and Worcestershire sauces
4 stuffed green olives, sliced

Soak gelatin in cold water. Mix hot water with bouillon granules. In 2-quart mixing bowl, add gelatin to hot bouillon; cool.

Add cream cheese to liver sausage, mayonnaise, onion, and sauces; mix in blender or with electric mixer. Add gelatin and bouillon; continue to blend.

Pour into 3½-cup mold that has been lightly oiled. Refrigerate. Garnish with sliced olives just before serving. Good served cold on brown bread or crackers.

Hint: *If using egg beater, mix liverwurst combination by spoon first; then add bouillon-gelatin mixture ½ cup at a time and beat until well blended.*

The table is the only place where the first hour is not dull.

Jean-Anthelme Brillat-Savarin
La Physiologie du goût, 1825

Betty Baker
Libby, Montana
Libby Dam Good Sams

Betty's "finger food" couldn't be easier, and when offered on a pretty platter it is perfect party fare.

Serves 12

Onion Rollups

1 dozen green onions
1 8-ounce package cream cheese, room temperature
1 2.5-ounce package pastrami, ham, or turkey

Clean and cut green onions into 4-inch lengths; for a special look leave some of the green ends longer to use as "handles" to pick up the appetizer.

Spread the cream cheese very carefully over each slice of meat or turkey. Place one green onion at one end of the slice of meat and roll up jelly roll fashion. Repeat with remaining onions and meat. Arrange on platter and serve.

Hint: Add grated cheddar cheese to the cream cheese for a delicious variation.

Irene L. Tujague
Thousand Oaks, California
Past Presidents Sams

This terrific recipe is almost too good to be true. The entire snack is prepared in a self-sealing plastic bag, and it's perfect for just about any occasion: a fishing outing, picnic, or Good Sam gathering.

Serves 10

Oysterette Snacks

1 12-ounce box oysterette crackers
1 cup vegetable oil
1 .04-ounce package ranch-style dressing mix
1/4 cup grated Parmesan cheese
1/2 teaspoon garlic powder
1/2 teaspoon dillweed

Place crackers in large self-sealing plastic bag. Pour in oil and turn from side to side until all crackers are moistened. Mix dry ingredients together and pour into bag. Seal tightly and turn from side to side until crackers are coated with seasonings.

Sharon McConnell
Bonita, California
Sandpiper Sams

When Sharon served her unusual
creation at the Southern California
State Samboree Cook-off, she was
swamped with requests for her
recipe. Now Good Samers everywhere
can enjoy this creative snack.

Serves 14

Spinach Tortilla Rollups

| 6 green onions, finely chopped |
| 2 tablespoons finely chopped cilantro (optional) |
| 1 tablespoon finely chopped parsley |
| 1 3-ounce can real bacon bits |
| 1 cup mayonnaise |
| 1 cup sour cream |
| 1 .04-ounce package ranch-style dressing mix |
| 2 10-ounce packages chopped frozen spinach, thawed and drained |
| 8 flour tortillas |

In large bowl, mix onions, cilantro, parsley, bacon bits, mayonnaise, sour cream, and dressing mix. Tear spinach into pieces and add to mixture; mix well.

Spread ⅛ of mixture over each tortilla; roll up, leaving ends open. Slice into bite-size pieces before serving.

Hint: These are delicious when warm. Pop rollups into microwave oven to heat just before serving.

Verlene Paquin
Elephant Butte, New Mexico
Sierra Sams

Verlene assures us it takes only 10 minutes to prepare this delightful salmon appetizer, and it works equally well with canned salmon or fresh salmon that has been baked or broiled.

Serves 12

Salmon Ball

1 16-ounce can salmon
1 8-ounce package cream cheese, softened
1 tablespoon lemon juice
½ teaspoon liquid smoke
1 teaspoon prepared horseradish
1 tablespoon grated onion
½ cup finely chopped nuts (optional)

In medium bowl, flake salmon; add cream cheese and mix. Add all other ingredients; mix well.

Form into ball; wrap in waxed paper. Refrigerate until firm. Place on serving plate and sprinkle with nuts, if desired. Serve with crackers.

Donna Lee McKenna
Omaha, Nebraska
Bug N Sams

Donna's unusual hors d'oeuvre contains pineapple and pecans in the cream cheese filling—a refreshing, crisp appetite whetter.

Serves 25

[handwritten:] DBL. made 80 pieces + cheeseball with extra — just refr. till it sets — Divit + roll in nuts

[handwritten:] Don't double recipe way too much ½ would make 40 pieces 2 each serve 20

"These Are Different" Celery Sticks

[handwritten note above table: 2½ inch pieces]

1 large bunch celery	3
1 8-ounce package cream cheese, room temperature	2
1 8½-ounce can crushed pineapple, well drained	2
½ cup chopped pecans	1
2 tablespoons finely chopped green pepper	4
1 tablespoon finely chopped onion	2
1½ teaspoons seasoned salt	+

Clean celery well. Cut each stick into 2½-inch pieces.

Mix together cream cheese, pineapple, nuts, green pepper, onion, and salt. Chill for several hours or overnight. Fill celery pieces with mixture and arrange on platter.

Hot Appetizers

Gene Schultz
White Bear Lake, Minnesota
Minnesota Skeeters

Gene's easy-to-fix appetizer will serve as many as you want—just measure out the correct amount of ingredients, allowing at least 2 per person.

Bacon-on-Breadsticks

Breadsticks, salted or unsalted
Bacon

Wrap a slice of bacon around each breadstick. Place wrapped breadsticks in a microwave baking dish. Small microwave ovens may require making several batches. Times will very according to your oven and the size of the dish you are using; small batches take about 5 minutes, large ones, about 10 minutes. For a conventional oven, bake at 350°F for 10 minutes. If you are using a conventional oven, you can precook the bacon and then wrap around breadsticks just before warming them up.

Rosemary Phillips
Winchester, Virginia
Shenandoah Sams

So easy to make in your microwave oven, Rosemary's savory wieners can be ready on a moment's notice.

Serves 8 to 10

Bourbon Wieners

1 pound all-beef wieners or cocktail-size wieners
1 cup catsup
³/4 cup bourbon
¹/2 cup firmly packed brown sugar

Cut the wieners into bite-size pieces, about 8 pieces to a regular-size wiener. Set aside.

Mix together the catsup, bourbon, and brown sugar in a 1¹/2-quart baking dish. Cover with waxed paper and microwave on high 3 minutes or until mixture boils. Add wieners and microwave on high 4 to 5 minutes or until hot. Serve wieners in chafing dish and provide toothpicks for guests to spear them.

Janet Tasker
Bozeman, Montana
Gallatin Good Sams
Big Sky Good Sams

Janet makes these savory morsels
ahead of time, freezes them on a
cookie sheet, and then removes them
to smaller freezer bags for longer
storage. When she's ready to serve
them, she removes just what she
needs and bakes them according to
the instructions.

Serves 12

Cheese Delights

Dough

2 cups flour

½ teaspoon cream of tartar

1 cup (2 sticks) butter

⅔ cup ice water

Filling

½ pound Monterey Jack cheese
with peppers or chilies, grated *or*

½ pound Monterey Jack cheese, grated
and mixed with 1 teaspoon parsley flakes

1 egg, slightly beaten

For dough: Combine flour and cream of tartar. Cut butter into small pieces and add to flour mixture. Cut into mixture with pastry blender or two knives until mixture is crumbly. Gradually add ice water. Mix well.

Divide dough into quarters. Wrap each piece in waxed paper or plastic wrap and refrigerate 1 hour. Remove 1 quarter of dough from refrigerator at a time, leaving remaining quarters until ready to roll.

For filling: Mix cheese with beaten egg.

For cheese delights: Roll out each quarter of dough, 1 quarter at a time, ¼ inch thick. Cut into small rectangles or circles. Place small amount of filling on each piece, dampen edges with water, fold over, and seal by pressing edges with tines of fork that have been dipped in flour. Prick top with tines of fork.

Place on ungreased cookie sheet and freeze, or bake at 425°F 12 to 15 minutes, until golden brown. Serve immediately.

Hint: If desired, brush lightly with milk or half and half before baking.

Virginia Hare
Baltimore, Maryland
Essex Pandas

*No need to look for those golden
arches when you can prepare
Virginia's chicken nuggets right in
your RV galley.*

Serves 14 to 16

Baked Chicken Nuggets

7 to 8 whole chicken breasts, skinned and boned
2 cups Italian bread crumbs
1 cup grated Parmesan cheese
1½ teaspoons salt
1 tablespoon plus 1 teaspoon dried whole thyme
1 tablespoon plus 1 teaspoon dried whole basil
1 cup (2 sticks) butter or margarine, melted

Preheat oven to 400°F.

Soak chicken breasts in salt water for several hours. Remove all bones and cut meat into 1½-inch pieces.

Combine bread crumbs, cheese, salt, and herbs and mix well. Dip chicken pieces in melted butter and coat with bread crumb mixture. Place on baking sheet in a single layer and bake 20 minutes or until done. Serve with dipping sauces, if desired.

Shirley Jairell
Laramie, Wyoming
Gem City Sams

*This appetizer that started out as
an hors d'oeuvre for a campground
happy hour is popular with
youngsters, too. Shirley created this
unusual snack when she was looking
through her RV galley for
something to take to a Good Sam
gathering. After a few refinements,
she decided to enter it in the
Wyoming State Samboree Cook-off,
where it came out a winner.*

Serves 10

Happy Hour Special

1 11-ounce package refrigerator biscuits
½ cup (1 stick) butter or margarine
2 cloves garlic, crushed
1 tablespoon sesame seeds

Preheat oven to 375°F.

Cut biscuits into quarters and place in 11 × 7-inch baking pan. Melt butter and stir in garlic. Pour over biscuit pieces, making certain that all are well covered. Sprinkle with sesame seeds. Bake 8 to 10 minutes or until biscuits spring back when lightly touched. Serve warm.

Hint: Parmesan cheese can be substituted for sesame seeds.

Gloria Loveday
Winnipeg, Manitoba,
Canada
Manitoba Goldeyes

You'll be popular around any campfire when serving Gloria's nachos treat. It's also a great snack while watching TV or taking a roadside rest.

Serves 8

Nachos Supreme

1 7½-ounce bag taco-flavored tortilla chips
1½ cups minced green pepper
1½ cups chopped tomatoes
1½ cups minced mushrooms
¾ cup minced celery
¾ cup minced onion
2 cups grated mild cheddar cheese

Preheat broiler to 500°F.

Coat cookie sheet with nonstick baking spray. Place layer of chips on cookie sheet; add layers of peppers, tomatoes, and mushrooms. Mix celery and onion together and sprinkle over other ingredients. Cover with cheese. Place under broiler 3 to 5 minutes or until cheese has melted. Serve hot.

Alta McNutt
Sierra Vista, Arizona
Cochise Renegades

Offer this crunchy snack with beverages, or pass around for TV watchers.

Serves 4 to 6

Spicy Pecans

1 pound pecans, shelled
½ cup (1 stick) margarine or butter, melted
Celery salt to taste
Garlic powder to taste, *or* 1 small clove garlic, minced
Cayenne pepper to taste
Salt and pepper to taste

Preheat oven to 200°F.

Toast the pecans on a baking sheet for 20 minutes, stirring every 5 to 10 minutes. Pour melted butter over pecans and toss thoroughly. Sprinkle on celery salt, garlic, cayenne, and salt and pepper to taste. Serve warm or at room temperature.

Cold Dips

Arthur Schaut, Jr.
Duarte, California
Semper Fi Sams

Art offers a mild or spicy version of his salsa. Serve with tortilla or corn chips.

Makes 3 to 4 cups

Art's Salsa

2 large bunches green onions, finely chopped

1 4-ounce can diced green chilies for milder flavor (Art prefers Ortega) *or*

1 3½-ounce can diced jalapeño peppers, for hotter flavor

1 4¼-ounce can chopped black olives

5 large tomatoes, diced

1 8-ounce bottle Italian salad dressing

Mix all ingredients in 1-quart bowl. Chill overnight.

Ruth Shake
Odon, Indiana
Cherokee Sams

Ruth layers the crabmeat over the filling in this subtly flavored dip. Great for serving with an assortment of crackers or fresh raw vegetables.

Serves 8 to 10

Crabmeat Dip

1 8-ounce package cream cheese, room temperature

2 tablespoons mayonnaise

2 tablespoons Worcestershire sauce

1 teaspoon lemon juice

1 small onion, minced

½ 12-ounce bottle chili sauce

1 6-ounce package frozen crabmeat, thawed, *or*

1 6-ounce can crabmeat

Chopped parsley for garnish

Mix first 5 ingredients together. Place on serving platter or dip plate. Pour chili sauce over cream cheese mixture. Sprinkle crabmeat over mixture and top with chopped parsley. Chill well before serving.

Mildred Smith
Orange, California
Lucky 13

Mildred's Fiesta Dip doesn't last long when she takes it to a camp-out happy hour.

Serves 8

Fiesta Dip

| 1 10½-ounce can bean dip |
| 2 ripe avocados, peeled, pitted, and mashed |
| 3 tablespoons mayonnaise |
| 3 tablespoons sour cream |
| ½ 1.25-ounce package taco seasoning mix |
| 1 4¼-ounce can chopped black olives |
| 1 bunch green onions, chopped, including tops |
| 1½ cups grated cheddar cheese |
| 2 large tomatoes, chopped |
| Salsa to taste (Mildred uses 30 drops) |

Spread bean dip over 12-inch serving plate. Combine avocados, mayonnaise, sour cream, and taco seasoning; blend well. Spread over bean dip. Layer with olives, onions, and cheese. Just before serving, add tomatoes and sprinkle with salsa. Serve with taco chips.

Karen Fisk
Agoura, California
Member at Large

Karen's interesting dip could be offered with fresh crudités—crisp, cold slices of raw cucumbers, green onions, broccoli, radishes, celery— and is at its best served at room temperature.

Serves 8

Jenny's Dip

| 1 8-ounce package cream cheese, room temperature |
| 1 8-ounce carton sour cream |
| 2 tablespoons milk |
| 2 tablespoons minced bell pepper |
| 2 tablespoons minced onion |
| 1 2½-ounce jar or package chipped beef, minced |

Have all ingredients at room temperature before starting. Mix until well blended. Serve with raw vegetables for dipping.

Jessie Payne Davis
Cameron Park, California
Member at Large

Jessie tells us that this recipe was used as a sandwich spread by her family during the depression. In those days, everything was cooked from scratch. Her mother even made her own mayonnaise and sour cream!

Serve 8 to 10

White Bean and Bacon Dip

1 11½-ounce can bean with bacon soup
½ cup mayonnaise
½ cup sour cream
2 tablespoons minced green onion
1 teaspoon seasoned salt
¼ teaspoon black pepper
½ teaspoon Tabasco sauce

Blend or beat soup until smooth. Add mayonnaise, sour cream, onion, and seasonings. Pour into a covered container and refrigerate. Serve as a dip or spread on homemade bread.

Lil Clark
Sparks, Nevada
Silver Sage Sams

Lil makes up several pints of her jalapeño jelly and serves it over cream cheese for a spicy party dip.

Makes 4½ pints

Jalapeño Jelly Camp-out Dip

7 jalapeño peppers, toasted and peeled, seeds removed
or
1 7-ounce can whole jalapeño peppers, seeds removed
1 green pepper, seeds removed, cut into squares
2 tablespoons fresh lemon juice
1½ cups cider vinegar
3½ cups sugar
1 6-ounce bottle liquid pectin
5 drops green food coloring
1 8-ounce package cream cheese

Mix all ingredients except sugar in blender and puree until smooth. Pour mixture into large saucepan and add sugar. Bring to boil and simmer 10 minutes. Remove pan from heat and add pectin and food coloring.

Divide into sterilized canning jars and seal. When ready to serve, pour one jar over cream cheese and accompany with crackers.

Hot Dips

Dee Miller
Cape May, New Jersey
Cape May Diamonds

This zippy dip can be prepared and served in a crockpot or fondue pot. Dee adds green chilies to give it extra pizzazz.

Serves 10 to 20

Dee's Hot Cheese Dip

| 1 pound sharp cheddar cheese |
| 1 pound processed cheese food spread (Dee likes Velveeta) |
| 1 16-ounce can whole tomatoes, well drained |
| 2 4-ounce cans chopped green chilies, drained |
| ¼ teaspoon garlic powder |

Cut cheeses into cubes and melt in crockpot or fondue pot. Cut up tomatoes and mix well with cheeses. Add chilies and garlic powder and stir gently until smooth. Heat until mixture is warm.

Audrey Renish
Joshua Tree, California
Joshua Jacks Sams

If you make Audrey's hot dip early in the morning and refrigerate, it's ready to pop in the oven when happy hour rolls around.

Serves 8

Hot Artichoke Dip

| 1 16-ounce can artichoke hearts in water, drained |
| 1 6-ounce jar marinated artichoke hearts, drained |
| 1 4-ounce can diced green chilies, drained |
| 8 to 10 tablespoons mayonnaise |
| 2 cups shredded sharp cheddar cheese |

Preheat oven to 350°F.

Chop artichokes and mix both varieties together. Place in shallow 2-quart baking dish or 8×8-inch pan. Sprinkle chilies over top. Spread mayonnaise over entire dish to seal. Sprinkle with shredded cheese. (Cover with plastic wrap and refrigerate if making ahead.)

To bake, place in preheated oven for 20 minutes until hot and bubbly. Recipe also can be microwaved on high 5 to 10 minutes. Serve with assorted crackers.

Betty Busse
Missoula, Montana
Garden City Sams

Refried beans and guacamole give Betty's dip a Mexican flavor. This would be a terrific appetizer for a south-of-the-border dinner.

Serves 6 to 8

Hot and Hearty Beef and Bean Dip

1 pound lean ground beef
1 2-ounce can green chilies
½ large onion, chopped
1 16-ounce can refried beans
1 pound cheddar cheese, grated
4 ounces guacamole dip, mixed with
1 cup sour cream

Brown ground beef in 12-inch skillet with chilies and onion. Drain fat. In an 8 × 10-inch baking pan, layer refried beans, ground beef, and grated cheese. Bake 15 minutes.

Remove from oven and spread the guacamole-sour cream mixture over top of ground beef mixture. Serve with Mexican-style chips or crackers.

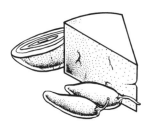

Being set at the table, scratch not thyself, and take thou heed as much as thou canst not to spit, cough and blow at thy nose; but if it be needful, do it dexterously, without much noise, turning thy face sidelong.

Francis Hawkins, *Youth's Behavior,* 1773

Beverages

Charles Vaughan
Cassville, Missouri
So-We-Mo Sams

Charles's punch has been used for years at family gatherings. It's especially good for camping because of the easy preparation.

Serves 15 to 20

Camper's Punch-out

1 12-ounce can frozen lemonade
1 cup sugar
1 32-ounce can cranapple juice
1 46-ounce can pineapple juice
1 2-liter bottle lemon-lime soft drink (such as 7-Up)

Mix the first 4 ingredients together. Just before serving add the lemon-lime drink. Serve over ice cubes or ice ring made with the fruit of your choice, such as pineapple cubes or green grapes.

Hint: Ingredients can be mixed up to a day before serving time, perhaps before leaving home for your outing. Then all you need to do is add the soft drink.

Geri Colwell
San Jose, California
Member at Large

Geri recommends her version of this popular drink. It's particularly convenient for RVers since the ingredients are easy to carry with you on the road.

Serves 4 to 6

Geri's Ramos Fizz

3 tablespoons instant orange drink (such as Tang)
2½ tablespoons confectioners sugar
3¼ cups ice cubes
¼ cup half and half
3 ounces vodka
1 egg

Mix all ingredients in blender and serve in frosted glasses.

Joseph Soares
Escalon, California
Ghost Riders

Joseph's inexpensive version of the higher priced coffee liqueur is every bit as good as the original.

Serves 12 to 15

Home-brewed Kahlua

6 cups water
5 cups sugar
7 tablespoons vanilla
2 ounces instant coffee, or preboiled regular coffee
1 quart vodka

Bring water to boil in saucepan. Add sugar and stir until dissolved. Add vanilla, coffee, and vodka. Remove from heat. Allow to cool.

When cool, pour into empty vodka bottle and seal. Serve over ice with or without cream for a great after-dinner drink.

Sybil Watts
Jackson, Mississippi
Dixieland Sams

What could be more inviting on a cold night than steaming cups of Sybil's Hot Apple Cider? It's so easy to prepare for a large crowd because it's made in a percolator.

Serves 30

Hot Apple Cider

5 short cinnamon sticks
2 teaspoons whole allspice
1 gallon apple cider
1 6-ounce can frozen orange juice, undiluted
2 2½-ounce packages red cinnamon candies (such as Red Hots)

Combine cinnamon sticks and allspice and place in the insert of a large (30-cup) percolator. Mix all other ingredients together and place in bottom of percolator. Let percolator cycle run through, just as you would when making coffee. Serve in mugs with cinnamon stick stirrers, if desired.

Marylou Montgomery
Fayetteville, North Carolina
Cape Fear Sams

While raising three sons and camping every weekend, Marylou found that she needed a hot drink that could be made up ahead of time and that was easy to store. She finally came up with the right combination of ingredients. Marylou and her husband still enjoy sharing their mix with other campers.

Makes approximately 40 cups (20 written above)
(10 cups of mix) (5 written below)

RVers' Hot Cocoa Mix

4 cups instant nonfat dry milk powder (2 handwritten)
3 cups nondairy creamer (1½ handwritten)
2½ cups granulated sugar (or sugar substitute equivalent) (1¼ handwritten)
⅔ cup cocoa (⅓ handwritten)
½ teaspoon salt (optional)

Mix all ingredients well in large mixing bowl. Store in airtight container.

When ready to use, put 4 tablespoons of cocoa mix in a cup, fill cup with hot water, stir, and enjoy. Top with a marshmallow, if desired.

Nola Taylor
Renton, Washington
Member at Large

What could be more refreshing than an icy glass of tea at the end of the road? Nola makes hers early in the day because it's better when it's allowed to sit for the flavors to combine.

Serves 8 to 10

Special Lemon Iced Tea

5 tea bags
6 cups boiling water
1 whole lemon
1 regular-size tray ice cubes

Use a large 10-cup bowl (a large mixing bowl with handle is great). Clip the tea bags to the side of bowl with a clothespin. With swivel-bladed vegetable peeler, pare off the yellow part of the lemon rind. Be careful not to include the bitter white part. Place lemon zest in bowl and pour boiling water over tea bags and lemon zest. Let stand 15 minutes or until tea is the desired strength. Squeeze out tea bags with kitchen tongs and discard.

Squeeze juice of the lemon into the tea. Add ice cubes. When cubes have melted, pour into covered pitcher and refrigerate 2 to 3 hours (leave the lemon zest in the tea).

When ready to serve, pour over ice in tall glasses. Sweeten according to taste.

Hint: *The longer the tea stands, the more lemony the taste.*

Phyllis Hadley
Ogden, Utah
Northern Utah Golden Spikers

Similar to a Bloody Mary, but
spicier and served hot, Phyllis's
before-dinner drink would be perfect
served at a Mexican dinner or on a
cold wintry day.

Serves 4

Spicy Mexican Cocktail

1 10½-ounce can condensed beef broth
2 cups vegetable juice
1 teaspoon lemon juice
½ cup vodka (optional)
Celery sticks for garnish

In a 1-quart saucepan, combine all ingredients except vodka and celery. Cover and cook over medium heat until heated through. Stir in vodka, if desired. Serve in mugs with celery-stick stirrers.

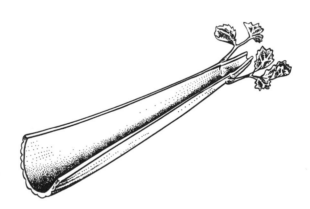

Now to the banquet we press; Now for the eggs and the ham! Now for the mustard and cress! Now for the strawberry jam! Now for the tea of our host! Now for the rollicking bun! Now for the muffin and toast! Now for the gay Sally Lunn!

W. S. Gilbert, *The Sorcerer*, 1877

Soups
and Salads

Soups

Cauliflower Chowder

Richard E. White
Roseburg, Oregon
Member at Large

Serve Richard's hearty chowder with chunks of fresh French bread for a satisfying meal.

Serves 4

2 tablespoons butter
2 tablespoons olive oil
1 large cauliflower, coarsely chopped
3 stalks celery, diced
3 medium carrots, diced
1 medium onion, chopped
½ green pepper, chopped
1 clove garlic, minced
4 cups water
4 chicken bouillon cubes
1 teaspoon seasoned salt
¼ teaspoon pepper
½ teaspoon dried dillweed

Melt butter in a 5-quart Dutch oven and add olive oil. Add vegetables and cook over medium heat until carrots are just tender. Add water and seasonings; simmer 15 minutes. Set aside 2 cups of the cooked chowder and puree remaining mixture in blender. Return both to Dutch oven and heat. Serve immediately.

Too many cooks spoil the broth.

Anonymous, English proverb

Olive Grubb
Clinton, Washington
Roamin' Wheels
Whid-Isle Sams

Olive has been making variations of this soup ever since she was old enough to reach the stove. It was a favorite of her children, and now her grandchildren ask her to make it. "Grandma always makes it better," they say. And, like most grandmothers, this is the first time Olive has measured out the ingredients.

Serves 4

Grandma Grubb's Potato Soup

2 cups cubed white potatoes (about 3 medium)
1 cup chopped yellow onion (about 1 large)
1½ cups water
1 teaspoon salt
2 strips bacon, diced
1½ cups milk
2 tablespoons butter

Put potatoes and onion in a 10-cup saucepan with water and salt. Cook over medium heat until the potatoes are very soft.

Brown bacon in small skillet. Drain and set aside.

When potatoes are soft, drain, and mash thoroughly with potato ricer. Return potatoes to pan and add milk. Cook over low heat until hot but not boiling. Add browned bacon and butter. Serve immediately.

Clara J. Riggs
Belen, New Mexico
Tumbleweeds of Albuquerque

Clara's easy-to-prepare soup is a creamy-spicy mixture that is both different and delicious. She begins her recipe, "First, you catch a chicken. . . ."

Serves 8 to 10

Chicken-Chili Soup

1 whole small chicken
6 cups chicken broth
1 10¾-ounce can cream of chicken soup
1 10¾-ounce can cream of celery soup
1 10¾-ounce can cream of mushroom soup
1 4-ounce can chopped green chilies
1 6- or 8-ounce package noodles, cooked
1 teaspoon salt
2 to 4 cups milk

In a 6-quart pot, boil chicken until tender. When cooled, remove meat from bones and cut into bite-size pieces. Mix together the chicken broth, cream soups, and chilies in a large pot. Add the cooked noodles and milk. Bring to boiling point, but do not boil. Serve immediately.

Hint: If you cook the chicken with some carrots, parsley, dillweed, onion, and celery, you will have homemade chicken broth for the soup. This broth can also be frozen for use in other dishes.

Ilene Norton
Springfield, Oregon
Member at Large

Ilene's hearty soup is filling and delicious. Serve with crisp breadsticks or crusty rolls.

Serves 6

Chilistroni

½ pound ground beef
3 cloves garlic, minced
½ cup chopped onion
½ cup sliced celery
1 28-ounce can tomatoes, cut into small pieces
1 10¾-ounce can beef broth
1 soup can water
2 teaspoons chili powder
1 15¼-ounce can kidney beans, undrained
2 medium zucchini, sliced
3 cups frozen mixed vegetables
Salt and pepper to taste
2 cups cooked macaroni

In a Dutch oven, brown beef, draining off fat. Add garlic and onion and sauté 1 minute. Add remaining ingredients, except macaroni. Cover and simmer 25 minutes. Add macaroni and simmer a few more minutes. If too thick, add a little more water to the soup.

Marian Hatch
Torrance, California
Member at Large

Marian often makes this creamy chowder when friends and neighbors come for dinner. Other than the basic clams, onions, and soups, ingredients can be varied according to what's in the pantry.

Serves 6 to 10

Creamy Clam Chowder

4 to 6 slices bacon, cut into ½-inch pieces
1 to 1½ cups diced onions
1 cup diced celery, including top leaves
½ cup diced green pepper (optional)
3 cups water
1 cup diced carrots
1 cup diced potatoes
1 6½-ounce can minced clams
1 10¾-ounce can clam chowder
1 10¾-ounce can cream of mushroom soup
1 10¾-ounce can cream of potato soup
1 10¾-ounce can cream of celery soup
1 8¾-ounce can cream-style corn
1 12-ounce can evaporated milk
3 cups water or milk
Salt and pepper to taste
Chopped green onion tops for garnish
Butter for garnish

In a large saucepan or kettle, sauté bacon until lightly browned. Remove to paper towel. Sauté onions, celery, and green pepper until soft and slightly cooked. Add water, carrots, and potatoes. Bring to boil and simmer until vegetables are crisp-tender. Add bacon, clams, soups, corn, evaporated milk, and water or milk. Bring to boil and simmer 20 minutes, stirring frequently to prevent scorching.

Serve in preheated soup bowls and top with green onions and butter, if desired.

Joan Bulkley
Humboldt, Arizona
Member at Large

This vividly colored Italian-seasoned soup makes a nutritious meal when served with whole wheat bread and a salad. The grain in the bread and the beans in the broth combine to give you your protein for the day. And what could be more comforting than a bowl of hot soup on a rainy day?

Serves 6 to 8

Rainy Day Minestrone

1 large yellow onion, diced
2 cloves garlic, minced
2 tablespoons olive oil
2 cups water
1 28-ounce can tomatoes
1 15¼-ounce can kidney beans
2 cups or more chopped vegetables, your choice, fresh or frozen
½ teaspoon Italian seasoning
½ cup elbow macaroni
2 cups fresh chopped zucchini
Salt and pepper to taste
Grated Parmesan cheese for garnish

Sauté onions and garlic in olive oil until limp. Add water, tomatoes, beans, vegetables (except zucchini), and Italian seasoning. Simmer 1 hour.

Add macaroni, zucchini, salt, and pepper and simmer an additional 30 minutes.

Serve in individual soup bowls and top with cheese.

There is no spectacle on earth more appealing than that of a beautiful woman in the act of cooking dinner for someone she loves.

Thomas Wolfe, *The Web and the Rock*

Roberta Kelley
Garden Grove, California
Member at Large

This flavorful soup, with a hint of the Old South, will make a complete meal when served with squares of fresh corn bread.

Serves 4 to 6

Quick RV Creole Chowder

2 tablespoons butter or margarine
1 16-ounce package frankfurters, cut in ½-inch slices
¼ teaspoon thyme
1 11½-ounce can split pea with ham soup
1 10¾-ounce can cream of potato soup
½ soup can water
1 8-ounce can tomatoes, cut into pieces
1 8-ounce can whole kernel corn, undrained

In large Dutch oven, melt butter. Add frankfurters and thyme and cook until browned. Pour in soups, then gradually stir in water. Add remaining ingredients and cook on medium heat until hot, stirring occasionally. Serve immediately.

Roberta Simmons
Poulsbo, Washington
Member at Large

This robust chowder would be perfect on a wintery night. Don't peel the potatoes, and you'll save time and nutrients. Roberta likes to serve it with fresh French bread.

Serves 6

Poulsbo-style Corn Chowder

4 medium boiling potatoes, unpeeled and cut into ½-inch cubes
1 pound bacon, cut in small pieces
2 12-ounce cans evaporated milk
1 16-ounce can cream-style corn, undrained
1 16-ounce can whole kernel corn, undrained
6 green onions *or* ½ medium yellow onion, cut into ½-inch pieces

In 4-quart soup pot, cover potatoes with water and boil until tender. Do not drain; set aside.

Fry bacon until crisp. Drain well.

Combine milk and undrained corn. Add onions, boiled potatoes in their cooking water, and bacon. Stir well and simmer on low heat 1½ hours (do not allow soup to boil), stirring occasionally. Serve hot.

Ivy M. Hjornevik
Austin, Texas
Armadillo Sams

Dried lentil beans give a rich and satisfying flavor to Ivy's delicious soup. Serve with a loaf of hot, whole wheat bread for a one-dish meal. This soup also freezes well, so it's perfect for traveling Good Samers.

Serves 6

Hearty Lentil Soup

1 12-ounce package lentil beans
2 quarts cold water
1 1.5-ounce package onion soup mix
1 bay leaf
1 cup chopped celery
1 cup diced carrots
2 cloves garlic, minced
¼ teaspoon pepper
2 tablespoons vegetable oil
½ pound lean sausage

In large kettle or stockpot combine all ingredients except sausage. Heat to boiling and then simmer, covered, 1 hour. Stir in sausage and cook an additional 30 minutes. Season with a little salt, if desired, before serving.

Rosemary H. Phillips
Winchester, Virginia
Shenandoah Sams

Rosemary's interesting soup is rich and thick. Serve with crusty, fresh bread, a salad, and some cheese for a satisfying meal.

Serves 6 to 8

White Bean Soup

1 pound white beans (pea or Great Northern)
6 cups cold water
1 teaspoon salt
1 meaty ham bone
1 tablespoon butter or margarine
½ cup chopped onion
Salt and pepper to taste

Place beans and water in large kettle and let stand overnight. When ready to cook, add salt and ham bone. Cover the kettle and bring to a boil. Simmer until beans are tender, about 1 to 1½ hours.

While beans are cooking, melt butter in small skillet and sauté onion over medium heat until transparent. Stir into beans and simmer. Add salt and pepper to taste.

When beans are tender, remove ham bone and let cool. Remove meat from bone and add to soup.

Hint: This can be made ahead of time and reheated when ready to serve. If soup has thickened, thin with a little water.

Margaret Poston
Baltimore, Maryland
Pleasure Seekers Sams

Knowing that her family liked bologna, Margaret started adding other favorite ingredients one day and came up with a triple treat soup that blends the flavor of bologna, tomatoes, and potatoes. It was a hit with the Postons, and it just might score a home run with the hearty appetites in your family.

Serves 20

Triple Treat Soup

4 28-ounce cans tomatoes, crushed in blender
2 28-ounce cans water
1 large onion, thinly sliced
3 tablespoons sugar
2 teaspoons salt
¼ teaspoon pepper
3 pounds bologna, sliced and quartered
6 large potatoes, peeled and cubed

In an 8-quart pot, cook tomatoes, water, onion, and seasonings over medium heat for 1 hour. Add bologna and potatoes and continue to cook until potatoes are tender. Remove lid and cook an additional 30 minutes.

Beautiful soup, so rich and green,
Waiting in a hot tureen!
Who for such dainties would not stoop?
Soup of the evening, beautiful soup!

Lewis Carroll,
Alice's Adventures in Wonderland, 1865

Shirley McGregor
Winnipeg, Manitoba, Canada
Manitoba Goldeyes

Shirley's version of this old Spanish summer soup is easy to prepare ahead of time. It is perfect hot-weather fare since the colder it is served, the better it is.

Serves 8 to 10

Gazpacho

5 large ripe tomatoes
2 large cucumbers *or* 1 long English cucumber
4 stalks celery, finely chopped
1 medium onion, finely chopped
3 to 4 broccoli florets, broken into smaller pieces
1 medium green pepper, finely chopped
½ 9¼-ounce jar olive salad with red peppers, chilled
1 teaspoon salt
⅛ teaspoon cayenne
3 tablespoons white vinegar
2 cups chilled tomato juice

Soak tomatoes in boiling water about 10 minutes. Peel and dice in small pieces. In a large bowl, combine tomatoes, cucumbers, celery, and onion. Add broccoli, peppers, and olive salad. Combine and slowly add seasonings and liquid ingredients.

Refrigerate for at least 6 hours before serving.

Hint: Great served in chilled bowls with croutons and ice cubes made of frozen tomato juice.

An unwatched pot boils immediately.

H. F. Ellis, *Punch*

*Marion A. Scott
Huntington Park,
California*
Long Beach Rollin'
Rigs Sams

*Looking for a hearty soup that's
good to the last drop? Try Marion's
tasty mélange of bacon, potatoes,
green beans, and wieners.*

Serves 4

Wiener Soup

2 strips bacon, diced
1 small yellow onion, chopped
2 cloves garlic, minced
3 cups water
3 cups peeled and diced potatoes
½ teaspoon salt
⅛ teaspoon pepper
¼ teaspon thyme
1 16-ounce can cut green beans
1 pound wieners, sliced 1 inch thick

In large skillet, cook bacon. Add onion and garlic; cook until translucent. Add next 5 ingredients; cook until potatoes are soft. Add green beans and liquid. Heat until blended. Coarsely mash ingredients with potato masher. Add wieners and reheat.

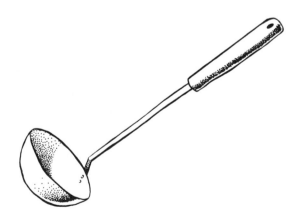

Vegetable Salads

Grace Almond
Englewood, Colorado
Member at Large

Grace's unusual first course dish, that is cooked and served chilled, differs from the Italian version. She serves it with celery sticks or on crisp crackers or melba toast squares.

Serves 6 to 8

Antipasto alla Grace

1 20-ounce bottle catsup

¼ cup cider vinegar

⅓ cup vegetable oil

1 teaspoon salt

1 teaspoon mustard

½ teaspoon creamed horseradish

2 large yellow onions, finely chopped

1 green pepper, finely chopped

1 red pepper, finely chopped

1 4-ounce can mushroom stems and pieces

2 16-ounce cans wax beans, drained and coarsely chopped

1 2¼-ounce can pitted ripe olives, chopped

1 2-ounce jar stuffed olives, drained and chopped

Combine all ingredients in a heavy 3-quart saucepan. Bring mixture just to a boil over medium heat. Remove from heat and transfer to a bowl to cool. When well cooled, place in refrigerator overnight to blend flavors.

Mildred S. Brown
Jersey City, New Jersey
Rolling Rovers

Mildred borrowed this recipe from her mother-in-law and finds it is popular with the potluck crowd at camp-outs. The ingredients are easily stored and it takes only minutes to prepare. It's a great accompaniment to barbecued hamburgers. It won first place in the New Jersey Samboree Cook-off.

Serves 6 to 8

Bean Salad Supreme

| 1 12-ounce can beans (Mildred prefers Campbell's Pork and Beans) |
| 1 cup diced green pepper |
| 1 cup diced celery |
| 1 cup diced yellow onion |
| ½ cup mayonnaise or to taste |

Mix first four ingredients together, add mayonnaise, and serve.

Hint: This dish can be heated before serving. For a nutritious and tasty luncheon salad, add cooked diced chicken.

Marie Mickey
Lompoc, California
Central Coast Sams

Marie's nutritious salad was a winner at the Nevada State Cook-off. Water chestnuts give it extra crunch.

Serves 12

Broccoli Salad

| 2 large bunches broccoli, finely chopped |
| 1 large red onion, finely chopped |
| 8 celery stalks, finely chopped |
| 1 8-ounce can water chestnuts, finely chopped |
| 1 4-ounce can chopped black olives |
| 2 tablespoons oregano |
| Cherry tomatoes (optional) |
| 1 16-ounce bottle Italian dressing (Marie prefers Kraft) |

Mix all ingredients together in a large bowl until well blended. Allow to stand for 2 hours until flavors mellow. (Salad can be kept in refrigerator several days.)

Florence Marshall
Taylor, Nebraska
Loup Valley Sams

Prepare Florence's salad before you hit the road, and you'll have time to enjoy your camp-out.

Serves 8 to 10

Campers' Potato Salad

6 red potatoes, boiled, peeled, and diced
5 eggs, hard-boiled and cut into small pieces
½ teaspoon salt
1 large tablespoon sugar
1½ tablespoons vinegar
1 teaspoon mustard
1 medium onion, finely chopped
2 to 3 tops from green onions, finely chopped
Pepper to taste
1 cup mayonnaise or salad dressing

Mix potatoes and eggs together. Then add remaining ingredients and mix to combine well. Add a little more mayonnaise if you like.

Hint: Boil potatoes with skins on, cool, and then peel.

June M. Taylor
Richmond, Virginia
Sundowner Sams

In searching for a low-calorie gelatin salad to take to a diet class, June came up with this cook-off winner recipe that has only 33 calories per ½-cup serving. It's also great for camp-outs because it can be prepared at home and will keep up to three days in the refrigerator.

Serves 8

Calorie Counter's Salad

2 0.3-ounce packages sugar-free lemon gelatin
1 cup boiling water
3 cups tomato juice
2 stalks celery, finely minced
1 small green pepper, finely minced
1 small onion, finely minced

In medium bowl, dissolve gelatin in boiling water; add tomato juice. Stir in vegetables. Chill until set.

Norma Campbell
Manchester, Iowa
Backbone Country Sams

Norma's make-ahead salad is great for RVers. It can be prepared in advance of a trip and will keep up to three weeks in the refrigerator. This was a first place winner in the salad category at the Iowa State Samboree Cook-off.

Serves 8 to 10

Everlasting Salad

1 quart water, salted with 1 tablespoon salt
1 medium head cabbage, shredded
2 large green peppers, diced
5 large carrots, grated
2 large sweet onions, diced
1 cup cauliflower florets
1 cup broccoli florets
2 cups sugar
2 cups vinegar
1 tablespoon celery seed
2 tablespoons mustard seed

Pour salted water over cabbage, peppers, carrots, onions, cauliflower, and broccoli. Let stand 2 hours; drain.

While vegetables are soaking, bring sugar, vinegar, celery seed, and mustard seed to boil; let cool. Pour over drained vegetables and store in refrigerator until needed.

Hint: *Before serving, add chopped pimientos for color.*

Barbara Burbach
Elizabeth, New Jersey
Rolling Rovers

Barbara's version of this all-time favorite is fast and tasty. Prepared Italian salad dressing mix makes it simple for RVers.

Serves 6 to 8

Hot German Potato Salad

6 slices bacon, cut into small pieces
2 medium onions, finely chopped
1 0.6-ounce package Italian salad dressing mix
5 pounds potatoes, boiled, peeled, and diced
4 eggs, hard-boiled and diced
Dash of Maggi seasoning

Fry bacon and ½ of the onions until bacon is crisp and onions are translucent.

Prepare salad dressing mix according to package directions.

Combine potatoes, eggs, raw onion, bacon, cooked onions with drippings, and seasoning. Add salad dressing and mix well. Serve warm.

Rosalie Schachterle
Vancouver, Washington
Member at Large

Molded salads have been in vogue since the turn of the century, and Rosalie's is as good for you as it is attractive.

Serves 4

Molded Vegetable Salad

1 3-ounce box lime gelatin
1 cup boiling water
1 tablespoon lemon juice
2 tablespoons finely chopped green pepper
1 tablespoon finely chopped onion
1 cup grated zucchini
1 cup grated carrots
1 cup applesauce
Lettuce leaves for garnish

Dissolve gelatin in boiling water. Add lemon juice and stir. Add remaining ingredients, stir well, and pour into mold. Refrigerate at least 3 hours before serving. Turn out onto lettuce leaves on platter.

Hint: Salad is at its best when you use the freshest, most crisp vegetables you can find.

Rosemary Phillips
Winchester, Virginia
Shenandoah Sams

The secret to Rosemary's salad is the dressing. She also finds the salad a great way to "clean out" her refrigerator. This is best made a day ahead.

Serves 10 to 12

Seven-Layer Salad

Salad

1 large head of lettuce, shredded
½ cup chopped green peppers
½ cup chopped or sliced green onions
1 pound frozen peas, rinsed and drained
½ cup chopped celery
1 8-ounce can water chestnuts, sliced
1 pound bacon, cooked and crumbled

Dressing

2 cups mayonnaise, preferably homemade
¾ cup sour cream
1 1.4-ounce package buttermilk salad dressing mix
Pinch of salt
Dash of Worcestershire sauce
Dash of hot pepper sauce
Dash of black pepper
Grated Parmesan cheese

For salad: Place ⅓ of shredded lettuce in a large glass bowl or trifle dish. (This will be your serving dish, so choose an attractive, clear container.) Layer the other vegetables over lettuce, adding the second ⅓ of lettuce at midpoint, and the remaining ⅓ of lettuce last. Sprinkle the bacon over top.

For dressing: Mix the mayonnaise, sour cream, salad dressing mix, salt, and seasonings together.

For finished dish: Spread the dressing mixture over the top of the salad, making sure to bring to edges to seal. Grate some Parmesan cheese over salad, cover with plastic wrap, and refrigerate overnight. You may prefer to toss before serving, but Rosemary feels this ruins the effect; just serve with tongs and the dressing will mix with the salad as it is served.

Betty Condit
Grants Pass, Oregon
Rogue River Rooster Sams

In the Minnesota town where Betty was born, there were many residents of German ancestry. Each year in October they held a "Sauerkraut Day," when everyone in town gathered together to share and eat recipes made with this ingredient—served along with meat dishes, cider, and other harvest goodies. This is one of those recipes.

Serves 8

Sauerkraut Calico Salad

1 16-ounce can sauerkraut, or fresh, if available
1 medium onion, chopped
1 medium green pepper, chopped
½ cup vinegar
¼ cup vegetable oil
1 teaspoon garlic salt
1 teaspoon celery seed
½ cup sugar
1 teaspoon salt
1 teaspoon pepper
1 cup chopped celery
1 cup shredded carrots

Wash the sauerkraut thoroughly until all odor is gone. Drain. Combine sauerkraut, onion, and green pepper. Set aside.

Combine remaining ingredients and pour over sauerkraut mixture. Stir well, cover, and refrigerate for at least 24 hours. This is even better the third day!

Sauerkraut and bacon drive all care away.

Anonymous, Pennsylvania Dutch proverb

Murdale Korleski
Arlington, Texas
Arlington Sams

Be sure to make Murdale's salad the same day it is to be served. Store in an airtight container to keep crisp. Everyone loves spinach salad, and this tasty version will round out the most ordinary meal.

Serves 8 to 10

Raw Spinach Salad

Salad

1 bag or bunch of fresh spinach, washed and torn in bite-size pieces

1 8-ounce can water chestnuts, drained and sliced

1 14-ounce can bean sprouts, drained, *or* ¾ pound fresh

3 eggs, boiled and diced

8 strips bacon, crisply fried and crumbled

Dressing

1 cup oil

⅓ cup catsup

1 medium-size white onion, grated

¼ cup wine vinegar

¼ cup sugar

2 tablespoons Worcestershire sauce

Salt and pepper to taste

For salad: Mix all vegetables together and add egg and bacon.
For dressing: Combine all ingredients and chill before using.
For finished salad: Pour dressing over salad just before serving.

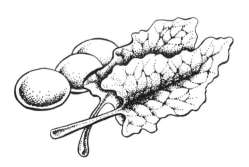

Harland O'Rear
Nevada, Missouri
Fun Seekers Sams

This delicious cole slaw recipe has been in Harland's family for more than 70 years since his grandmother first made it. It's simple to prepare and would be great for potlucks and Samborees.

Serves 8

Old-fashioned Cole Slaw

1 small head cabbage
⅓ cup sugar
2 tablespoons vinegar
2 tablespoons mayonnaise or salad dressing
1 small onion, minced
½ teaspoon paprika
½ teaspoon celery seed
Pinch of salt
Paprika for color

Chop cabbage into finely cut pieces using hand chopper or food processor. Mix sugar, vinegar, and mayonnaise together until thoroughly blended.

Pour mixture over chopped cabbage and combine well. Add minced onion, celery seed, and salt. Mix again. Sprinkle paprika over top for color and cover and refrigerate until ready to serve.

That all-softening overpowering knell
The tocsin of the soul—the dinner bell.

George Gordon, Lord Byron, *Don Juan,* 1821

Main-Course Salads

Helen Kost
Rogue River, Oregon
Rogue River Roosters Sams

Helen's salad can serve as a main course for a light dinner or lunch. It's simple to prepare and will delight crab lovers.

Serves 4

Crab Pasta Salad

4 cups water
1 teaspoon salt
1 teaspoon cooking oil
2 cups curly noodles, uncooked
³⁄₄ cup crabmeat, chopped
3 green onions, diced, including some of the tops
1 large stalk celery, diced
¹⁄₄ cup sliced black olives
¹⁄₃ cup mayonnaise
¹⁄₄ cup half and half or milk
Salt and pepper to taste
1 egg, hard-boiled, sliced
¹⁄₂ large tomato, sliced or cut in chunks

In a 4-quart kettle, bring water, salt, and cooking oil to boil. Add noodles and cook 10 minutes. Drain in colander, rinse under cold water, and transfer to bowl.

Add crabmeat, onions, celery, and olives and mix well.

In a small bowl, mix mayonnaise, half and half, salt, and pepper. Add dressing to salad and toss lightly. Refrigerate until ready to serve. Decorate with sliced egg and tomato pieces.

Hint: For a more economical version, imitation crab can be used.

Charlotte L. Ansalvish
Elkton, Maryland
First Staters Sams

Mix up this zesty salad at home and let it chill in the RV refrigerator on the way to your next camp-out. You'll be sure to see lots of people coming back for refills.

Serves 6 to 8

Spaghetti Salad

1 pound long, thin spaghetti (uncooked)
1 tomato, coarsely chopped
1 medium onion, finely chopped
1 green pepper or sweet banana pepper, diced
1 3.12-ounce bottle salad topping
1 0.6-ounce package Italian salad dressing mix

Break spaghetti into thirds; cook as directed on package; rinse in cold water; drain. Mix together chopped tomato, onion, and pepper. Add salad topping and mix. Prepare Italian salad dressing according to directions on package. Pour over salad and refrigerate. Serve cold.

Hint: Charlotte prefers to use McCormick's salad topping and Good Seasons Zesty Italian salad dressing mix.

No man is lonely while eating spaghetti.

Robert Morley

Charlotte Stockbridge
Granger, Indiana
Fun Lovin' Sams

The versatility of Charlotte's salad
will make it one of your most used
recipes. Any type of pasta will do,
and tuna can be substituted for the
salmon. What's more, it can be
served hot or cold.

Serves 4

Salmon Pasta Salad

4 tablespoons corn oil
1 medium onion, finely chopped
1 medium red pepper, finely chopped
1 teaspoon thyme leaves
½ teaspoon oregano leaves
1 7½-ounce can pink salmon, boned, flaked, and drained
1 cup uncooked pasta (noodles, rotini, shells, stars)
⅔ cup grated Parmesan cheese
Freshly ground pepper

Heat 2 tablespoons of the oil in a heavy 10-inch skillet. Sauté onion and pepper with thyme and oregano until softened. Add salmon and remove from heat. Set aside.

Cook noodles according to package directions, adding 2 tablespoons oil to water. Drain and toss with ½ of cheese until coated. Add salmon mixture and toss lightly. Season with ground pepper and top with remaining cheese. Serve warm or chilled.

Hint: Green pepper may be substituted for red; add 1 tablespoon pimiento for color.

According to the Spanish proverb, four persons are wanted to make a good salad: a spendthrift for oil, a miser for vinegar, a counselor for salt, and a madman to stir it all up.

Abraham Hayward, *The Art of Dining*, 1952

Margaret Adamson
Hallock, Minnesota
Prairie Rose Sams

*Margaret's first prizewinning salad
is a welcome change from
conventional ones, and since it uses
all fresh vegetables, it's nutritious,
too. A terrific main dish for a
luncheon, it can be prepared the
night before and refrigerated
until time to pull over at a scenic
rest stop.*

Serves 12

Vegetable Pizza Salad

1 8-ounce package refrigerator crescent rolls
1 8-ounce package cream cheese
¾ cup salad dressing (Margaret prefers Miracle Whip)
1 .04-ounce package ranch-style dressing mix
3 teaspoons finely chopped onion
1 cup finely chopped broccoli
1 cup finely chopped celery
1 cup finely chopped cauliflower
½ cup sliced green stuffed olives
½ cup sliced ripe olives
1 cup mild shredded cheddar cheese

Preheat oven to 350°F.

Unroll rolls, spread on bottom of 9 × 13-inch baking pan, and prick with fork. Bake for 15 minutes or until light brown.

Mix together cream cheese, salad dressing, dressing mix, and onion. Spread on cooled prepared crust. Toss together broccoli, celery, cauliflower, and both kinds of olives; sprinkle over dressing. Spread cheese over top. Cut into squares and serve on salad plates.

Hint: For best results, use only fresh vegetables. If preparing in advance, cover with foil and store in refrigerator.

Lettuce, like conversation, requires a good deal of oil, to avoid friction and to keep the company smooth.

Charles Dudley Warner, *My Summer in a Garden*, 1871

Winifred A. Bowles
Indianapolis, Indiana
Indy Sams

Winifred recommends making this salad the day before a potluck and adding the lettuce right before serving. Arranged in an attractive bowl, it will be the star attraction.

Serves 4 to 6

Tuna-Shell Salad

2 cups cooked shell macaroni, well rinsed and drained

1 7-ounce can tuna, drained

½ cup frozen peas, thawed and drained

2 eggs, hard-boiled and chopped

½ cup cubed cheddar cheese

2 tablespoons finely chopped onion

3 tablespoons chopped dill pickle

½ teaspoon lemon pepper

½ cup mayonnaise

Lettuce leaves (optional)

Combine all ingredients (except lettuce) and toss lightly. Refrigerate overnight. Serve on lettuce leaves or in pretty bowl.

Dorothy Bond
Nashville, Indiana
Scenic Sams

Dorothy's yummy pasta salad makes a meal by itself. It also adds color to a potluck table, but won't last long once Good Samers taste it—the recipe won third place in the Kentucky State Samboree Cook-off.

Serves 6

Mama Mia Salad

1 8-ounce package pasta (Dorothy prefers Creamette Rainbow Rotini)

1 5-ounce can chunk white chicken

1 cup chopped tomato

1 cup chopped cauliflower

½ cup chopped green pepper

½ cup chopped white onion

½ cup grated or diced cheese (your choice)

Italian dressing (Dorothy prefers Henri's Italian dressing)

Prepare pasta according to directions on package; drain and rinse with cold water. Add next 6 ingredients to pasta. Toss with Italian dressing. Cover and chill until served.

Jewel B. Teague
Lakeland, Florida
Silver Sams

If you are on the road, Jewel's salad is easy to prepare and needs little else to make a complete meal.

Serves 8

Jewel's Taco Salad Dinner

1 pound ground beef
1 head lettuce, torn into small pieces
3 tomatoes, chopped
1 onion, coarsely chopped
8 ounces cheddar cheese, grated
1 6-ounce package corn chips, broken into pieces
½ cup taco sauce
Salt and pepper to taste
Hot sauce
1 10-ounce can of vegetables (beans, corn, or your choice)

Brown ground meat in a 12-inch skillet. Drain well.

Mix lettuce, tomatoes, and onions. Add cheese and chips. Set aside.

Mix ground beef with taco sauce and add to vegetables. Toss well and serve immediately. Pass hot sauce and salt and pepper for those who like a little extra zip.

Hints: Summer sausages can be sustituted for the cooked ground beef. The ground beef also can be cooked and drained at home, placed in self-sealing bags and frozen. This makes on-the-road meal preparation even easier.

Lena Czerwonka
Ridgecrest, California
Sagebrush Sams

Lena's nutritious salad would be
perfect fare for a cool summer lunch
or Sunday dinner. Round out with
hot rolls and iced tea.

Serves 6 to 8

Woolly Worm Salad

3 quarts water

1 tablespoon oil

3 cups dry pasta twists

1 6-ounce jar marinated artichokes, drained and cut into quarters, liquid reserved

1 2¼-ounce can sliced black olives, drained

2 tablespoons chopped pimiento

⅓ cup chopped celery

1 small zucchini, chopped, unpeeled

½ cup chopped onion

½ cup chopped green pepper

½ cup Italian dressing (Lena prefers Wishbone Robusto)

Bring water and oil to boil in large saucepan, adding a little salt if desired. Add pasta and cook 10 minutes. Drain and rinse with cold water; drain again. In large bowl, combine pasta, artichokes, olives, pimiento, celery, zucchini, onion, and green pepper. Mix well and add salad dressing and marinade from artichokes. Mix again and store in covered bowl in refrigerator. When ready to serve, arrange on chopped lettuce in bowls. Add more dressing, if desired.

Salad refreshes without weakening and comforts without irritating.

Jean-Anthelme Brillat-Savarin
La Physiologie du goût, 1825

Vivian Ross
Alburquerque, New Mexico
The Romas Sams
Tumbleweed Sams

Vivian's light, refreshing salad would look pretty served in scooped-out papaya shells and offered as a delightful brunch dish.

Serves 6 to 8

Shrimp Salad

Salad
2 cups small elbow macaroni, cooked and cooled
1 small onion, finely chopped
½ cup chopped celery
1 to 2 4½-ounce cans shrimp, drained, or fresh, if available
3 eggs, boiled, peeled, and diced

Dressing
½ cup salad dressing
½ cup sweet pickle juice
½ teaspoon mustard
½ teaspoon thyme (optional)

For salad: Mix all ingredients together.
For dressing: Mix all ingredients well and pour over salad. Refrigerate until ready to serve.

Hint: One can of shrimp may be all that you need. If you have more people than you planned for, add another cup of cooked macaroni.

Salad Dressings

Mildred Ripplinger
Rice Lake, Wisconsin
Member at Large

*An easy-to-make dressing to add zip
to any salad, Mildred adds celery
seed for that extra bit of flavor.*

Makes 1 quart

Celery Seed Dressing

1¼ cups sugar
2 teaspoons salt
2 teaspoons dry mustard
½ medium white onion, grated
1 cup plus 3 tablespoons vinegar
2 cups vegetable oil
2 tablespoons celery seed

Combine sugar, salt, mustard, onion, and ½ the vinegar. Gradually add oil and continue beating. Beat in remaining vinegar in small amounts. Add celery seed and beat again until mixture is thick. Keep refrigerated.

Gladys Myers
Dauphin, Manitoba, Canada
Parkland Sams

*Gladys's dressing is easy to make
with ingredients on hand. She
suggests varying the amount of
sugar according to your family's
taste.*

Makes about 3½ cups

Gladys's Choice Dressing

1 large onion, finely chopped
¾ cup sugar
½ cup vinegar
1 cup catsup
¾ cup oil
1 teaspoon Worcestershire sauce
1 tablespoon chili sauce
Garlic powder to taste

Mix all ingredients in a 1-quart covered jar. Shake well and refrigerate. This will keep indefinitely.

Eleanor M. Miltner
Sheridan, Wyoming
Bot Sots Good Sams

Eleanor makes her dressing in a blender, but it can be prepared using a rotary beater, wire whisk, or by shaking vigorously in a sealed container. Any way you choose, it's bound to make your salad special.

Makes 3 cups (40 servings)

Sassy French Dressing

1 10¾-ounce can tomato soup

¾ cup salad oil

¾ cup vinegar

¾ teaspoon salt

1 tablespoon Worcestershire sauce

1 tablespoon dry mustard

1 tablespoon grated onion

Dash garlic powder

1 tablespoon unflavored gelatin

1 cup sugar

Swirl all ingredients in blender or mix with rotary beater or wire whisk. Shake well before serving.

Merle E. Freeman
Durant, Oklahoma
Texoma Sams

Merle recommends using this dressing on shredded lettuce, purple cabbage, and thinly sliced onions for a deliciously different salad or side dish.

Makes ¾ pint

Old Naples Italian Dressing

1 cup olive oil, room temperature

⅓ cup lemon juice, concentrated or fresh

⅓ cup apple cider vinegar

½ teaspoon Tabasco sauce

½ teaspoon garlic powder

½ teaspoon salt

½ teaspoon black pepper

1 teaspoon parsley flakes

Mix olive oil, lemon juice, vinegar and Tabasco in a 1-pint jar with lid. Shake vigorously. In separate small bowl, mix all dry ingredients together and add to liquid. Shake again and refrigerate for at least 30 minutes before using.

Carolyn M. Swalling
Charlo, Montana
Member at Large

This recipe was given to Carolyn by Lillian Summers, who managed a café when Carolyn knew her. At different times, she has added variations to the basic ingredients, but feels the original is still best. Terrific on fresh vegetable salad!

Makes 4 cups

Lillian Summers's French Dressing

1 cup sugar
1 cup vegetable oil
1 cup catsup
½ cup cider vinegar
½ cup red wine tarragon vinegar
1 teaspoon dried parsley
1 teaspoon salt
¼ teaspoon pepper
Dash paprika
⅓ teaspoon Worcestershire sauce

Combine all ingredients in a shaker jar and mix well. Refrigerate for at least 24 hours to blend seasonings. Shake well before serving.

Hint: In her camping trailer, Carolyn makes ¼ the recipe so that she can store it in the smaller refrigerator.

To make a good salad is to be a brilliant diplomatist—the problem is entirely the same in both cases. To know how much oil one must mix with one's vinegar.

Oscar Wilde, *Vera, or the Nihilists,* 1880

Marjorie Ross
Paragon, Indiana
Indy Sams

Marjorie felt that most vinegar-oil dressings were flat and flavorless, so she came up with this piquant combination of spices to make the most ordinary salads come to life. Since she is asked to bring the salads to most of the Indy Sams's potlucks, she has earned a reputation as an expert salad maker.

Makes about 1½ cups
(enough for 1 head of lettuce)

Spicy Garlic Dressing

1 cup sugar
¼ cup apple cider vinegar
1 tablespoon cold water
1 teaspoon garlic salt
½ teaspoon onion salt
½ teaspoon celery salt
1 teaspoon seasoned salt (Marjorie prefers equal portions of Lawry's and Aunt Jane's Crazy Salt)
¼ teaspoon black pepper
¼ teaspoon celery seed
½ cup vegetable oil (approximate)

Mix all ingredients except oil together and set aside for several hours to let the flavors combine. Then measure mixture in measuring cup and add ½ as much oil as you have sugar/vinegar mixture. Refrigerate for several hours before serving.

Sally Peterson
Dunning, Nebraska
Loup Valley Sams

This creamy version of an old favorite will make a large amount for a potluck or Samboree contribution. Sally uses an electric mixer to ease the preparation.

Makes 1 quart

Sally's Blue Cheese Dressing

2 cups mayonnaise
1 cup vegetable oil
1½ tablespoons wine vinegar
⅓ teaspoon garlic powder
¼ pound blue cheese, crumbled

Place mayonnaise in large bowl of electric mixer. On low speed, alternately add oil and vinegar. Add garlic powder and continue mixing. Remove bowl from mixer and add blue cheese. Pour into covered container and refrigerate.

Fruit Salads

Clint D. Goad
Durant, Oklahoma
Texoma Sams

Clint's salad is perfect for camp-outs and RVers in general— almost everything can be stored on the shelf.

Serves 12

Campers' Fruit Salad

1 3½-ounce package instant banana pudding mix (do not use regular pudding)
1 16-ounce can apricot halves, drained, juice reserved
3 medium bananas, sliced
1 16-ounce can pineapple chunks, drained
1 11-ounce can mandarin oranges, drained
1 cup miniature marshmallows
½ cup chopped pecans
1 cup fresh seedless grapes (white or red)

Combine pudding mix and apricot juice until smooth. Fold in bananas.

Cut apricots in half and add to mixture. Add pineapple chunks and oranges. Fold in marshmallows, pecans, and grapes. Chill for several hours before serving.

Hint: Toss bananas in pudding-juice mixture as soon as sliced to prevent them from darkening. Fresh diced pears can be substituted for the grapes.

The flesh of the pineapple melts into water and it is so flavorful that one finds in it the aroma of the peach, the apple, the quince and the muscat grape. I call it with justice the king of fruits because it is the most beautiful and best of all those of the earth.

Père du Tertre, 1595

Shirley A. Wilkinson
Wilmington, Illinois
Prairie State Sams

Shirley's creamy fruit salad was a winner at the Michigan State Samboree Cook-off. Serve with chicken or ham for an easy busy-day dinner.

Serves 6 to 8

Pineapple-Orange Salad

1 3½-ounce package instant or
1 0.8-ounce package sugar-free vanilla pudding mix

1 0.3-ounce package sugar-free orange gelatin

1 20-ounce can pineapple chunks with juice

1 8-ounce container whipped topping

1 cup miniature marshmallows

6 maraschino cherries

Mix together the pudding and gelatin. Fold in pineapple, juice, and whipped topping. Add marshmallows and stir well.

To serve, divide into equal portions on lettuce leaves and top each serving with a cherry.

Nita Clayton
Del Rio, Texas
Amistad Sams

When Nita's children were little, they would ask her to make "the pink salad." Adults will enjoy it too—it's so easy to fix.

Serves 6

Pink Salad

1 3-ounce package lemon gelatin

½ cup boiling water

1 3-ounce package cream cheese

1 4-ounce bottle maraschino cherries,
chopped, undrained

1 cup crushed pineapple

¾ cup chopped nuts (optional)

1 cup whipping cream (whipped), or whipped topping

Dissolve gelatin in boiling water. Add cream cheese and mix until well blended. Let cool slightly, then add chopped cherries and juice, pineapple, and nuts. Chill until slightly thickened. Fold in whipped cream and pour into an oiled salad mold, individual molds, or a bowl. Refrigerate several hours before serving.

Patricia Jackson
Anchorage, Alaska
Sourdough Sams

The combination of strawberries, pineapple, and nuts in Patricia's salad make an appetizing accompaniment to poultry or meats.

Serves 12

Strawberry Nut Salad

2 3-ounce packages strawberry gelatin
1 cup boiling water
2 10-ounce packages frozen strawberries, thawed, juice reserved (or fresh, if available)
1 20-ounce can crushed pineapple, drained
2 medium bananas, mashed
1 cup chopped nuts
2 cups sour cream
Lettuce leaves for garnish

Dissolve gelatin in boiling water in large bowl. Fold in strawberries with juice, drained pineapple, bananas, and nuts.

Pour ½ of mixture into a 12 × 8-inch dish. Refrigerate until firm. Spread sour cream over top and gently spoon remaining strawberry mixture over sour cream layer. Refrigerate several hours. Cut and serve squares on lettuce leaves if desired.

Zola Malamen
Anoka, Minnesota
Minnesota Voyagers

Just a few minutes and Zola's sour-cream-coated grape salad is ready to serve. It would be perfect for a summer lunch.

Serves 6

White Grape Salad

3 cups white seedless grapes (or green, if white are unavailable)
6 tablespoons sour cream
6 whole lettuce leaves, washed and drained
6 teaspoons brown sugar
6 maraschino cherries (with stems, if available)

Wash grapes and drain. Place in medium bowl and stir in sour cream.

Chill lettuce leaves and grape-sour cream mixture in refrigerator until ready to serve.

To serve, spoon ½ cup of grape mixture onto a lettuce leaf. Sprinkle 1 teaspoon brown sugar over grapes and top with a cherry. Repeat for other 5 servings.

Donna Lee McKenna
Omaha, Nebraska
Bug N Sams

This tasty fruit treat is good anywhere . . . for a picnic or RV barbecue, or just by itself for a summer lunch. Donna suggests adding fresh strawberries when in season.

Serves 8

Pretty Easy Fruit Salad

1 20-ounce can pineapple chunks, drained (reserve liquid)
1 16-ounce can chunky mixed fruit, drained
1 pint fresh strawberries, cleaned and halved
1 3½-ounce package instant vanilla pudding mix
2 bananas, sliced

Combine pineapple chunks, fruit, and strawberries in bowl that has been lined with paper towels to absorb excess juice. Refrigerate.

Prepare dressing by combining dry pudding with reserved pineapple liquid; mix well and refrigerate until chilled and thickened.

Combine dressing mixture, canned fruit, and strawberries; carefully fold in bananas. Refrigerate until ready to serve.

A grapefruit is a lemon that had a chance and took advantage of it.

Anonymous

Breads

Honorable Mention

Phyllis York
Gorham, Maine
Pinecrafters Sams

These light and flaky cook-off winning biscuits are delicious with a hearty breakfast or served with a large platter of fried chicken. They'll melt in your mouth.

Serves 12

Bakewell Cream Biscuits

4 cups flour
4 teaspoons Bakewell Cream*
1 teaspoon salt (may be omitted)
2 teaspoons baking soda
1¾ cups milk
½ cup mayonnaise

Preheat oven to 400°F. Mix and sift dry ingredients together. Add milk and mayonnaise; mix. Turn out onto floured board; knead 5 or 6 times. Cut with biscuit cutter. Bake 10 minutes, then lower heat to 325°F until biscuits are golden.

Hint: *You can turn off oven heat after 10 minutes; the biscuits will still brown.*

*If in an area where Bakewell Cream is not available, order by mail from Byron H. Smith & Co., Inc., 54 Perry Road, P.O. Box 875, Bangor, Maine 04401. Send $2 for each box plus $1.75 handling and postage.

Marie E. Houmes
Stone Mountain, Georgia
Carefree Sams

Marie believes in making the healthiest foods possible for her family. Blue cornmeal, high in the amino acid lysine, is the essential ingredient in this delicious and nutritious bread. Look for the cornmeal in health stores if not available in your market.

Blue Corn Bread

1 cup blue cornmeal
1 cup enriched flour
⅓ cup sugar
1 teaspoon salt
1 teaspoon baking powder
2 eggs
⅓ cup corn oil
1 cup milk

Preheat oven to 450°F.
Sift dry ingredients together.

In small bowl mix eggs, oil, and milk. Add dry ingredients to the liquid and mix well. Spread in a greased 9×9×2-inch baking pan and bake 20 to 25 minutes or until browned on top and pulling away from sides of pan.

Golden Bread

Shirley Hartmann
Libby, Montana
Libby Dam Good Sams

Shirley credits her husband's 40-pound weight loss and ability to keep it off to this bread. She says he eats it at every meal and sometimes before bed as a snack, toasted. Although we can't guarantee the same results for everyone, it's certainly nutritious and low in calories.

Makes 2 1½-pound loaves

2 cups instant uncooked hot cereal (Shirley prefers Zoom or Wheatena)
1 cup high fiber cereal (such as Fiber One or All Bran)
¼ cup reduced calorie margarine
¼ cup honey
2 teaspoons salt or salt substitute
2½ cups hot water
2 ¼-ounce packages dry yeast
5 to 5½ cups all purpose flour

Put cereals into a large bowl. Add margarine, honey, and salt. Pour in hot water and cool until lukewarm. Add yeast and allow to set about 5 minutes. Add flour and combine well. Turn out onto lightly floured surface. Knead until smooth and elastic, about 8 minutes. Form into rounded ball and place in greased bowl, turning bottom side to top. Cover and let rise in a warm place until doubled in bulk, about 1 hour. Punch dough down and allow to rise again, about 40 minutes.

Fashion into two equal loaves and place in 2 well-greased 9×5×3-inch loaf pans. Cover and allow to rise in a warm place until doubled, about 1 hour.

Preheat oven to 325°F. Bake loaves 1 hour.

***Hint:** These breads freeze well, so double the recipe and have loaves on hand when you need them. Also, use the reduced calorie margarine to grease the bread, bowl, and pans; it gives the bread a lovely golden color.*

Marylou Montgomery
Fayetteville, North Carolina
Cape Fear Sams

Marylou prepares these biscuits ahead of time and pops them in the freezer until the family is ready for a homemade treat. The biscuits are ideal for a quick breakfast or evening snack.

Makes 4 dozen

Biscuit Surprise

4 cups biscuit mix
1 cup milk
½ cup (1 stick) softened butter or margarine
1 pound ground sausage
1 cup grated cheddar cheese

In medium bowl, stir biscuit mix and milk with fork to form soft ball. Dough will be stiff and sticky. Turn out onto lightly floured board. Gently knead 8 to 10 times until smooth. Roll out dough into rectangular shape about ⅓ inch thick. Spread butter and then sausage over dough. Sprinkle with cheese. Roll up jelly roll fashion. Put roll on cookie sheet; cover with waxed paper and refrigerate 3 to 4 hours.

Remove from refrigerator and cut into ½-inch-thick slices. Place slices on cookie sheet. Cover with waxed paper and freeze. When biscuits are frozen, place in self-sealing plastic bags and return to freezer until ready to bake.

To bake, preheat oven to 400°F. Unwrap frozen biscuits and arrange on cookie sheet. Bake 15 to 20 minutes.

Norma Jeane Ross
Granite City, Illinois
Cardinal Sams

Norma Jeane uses the cheese spread on hamburger buns as well as split dinner rolls. Since it will keep in the refrigerator for two weeks, she can make it prior to a trip and have it on hand when needed.

Serves 12

Gooey Cheese Bread n' Spread

2 garlic cloves, crushed
2 cups shredded cheddar cheese
2 cups mayonnaise
1 bunch green onions, minced
1 French bread, split *or* 12 dinner rolls
Paprika (optional)

Preheat oven to 300°F.

Combine all ingredients except paprika. Spread on split French bread or rolls. Sprinkle with paprika. Bake 10 to 15 minutes, then broil 2 to 3 minutes, until cheese is bubbly.

T. Anne Marvel
Cornish, Maine
Pinecrafters

Anne whips up her popovers in a blender and puts them straight into a cold oven, but they come out golden brown and ready to eat.

Serves 6

Garlic-Butter Popovers

2 eggs
1 cup milk
1 cup flour
¼ teaspoon salt
½ cup (1 stick) butter or margarine, melted
¼ teaspoon garlic powder

Generously grease custard cups with shortening. In blender, beat eggs on mix cycle 5 seconds. Add remaining ingredients; mix 15 seconds. Do not overmix. Fill cups ¾ full. Place in cold oven. Set temperature at 400°F. Bake 50 minutes.

Hint: *Because there are only two of them, Anne uses custard cups. However, smaller popovers can be made in muffin tins.*

Margaret Freeman
Durant, Oklahoma
Texoma Sams

Remember sitting down to a meal with the family just as the corn bread was taken out of the oven? If the family is down to two, Margaret's recipe is just right for your RV dinners, with a little left over.

Serves 2

Corn Bread for Two

½ cup cornmeal
1 teaspoon sugar
¼ teaspoon salt
⅛ teaspoon baking soda
1 teaspoon baking powder
1 egg, well beaten
½ cup buttermilk
1 scant tablespoon bacon drippings

Preheat oven to 425°F.

Mix dry ingredients and add to beaten egg. Pour in buttermilk and stir just enough to incorporate. Stir in hot bacon drippings. Pour batter into hot, preferably cast iron, skillet. Bake 35 to 40 minutes or until golden brown.

Josephine Miller
Homestead, Florida
Silver Sams

Green tomatoes fried in cornmeal batter have been a staple in many Southern kitchens for years. Josephine's recipe calls for an unusual combination of the green tomatoes, raisins, currants, and chopped nuts to create a very different bread.

Makes 2 loaves

Green Tomato Bread

1 cup vegetable oil
2 cups sugar
1 teaspoon salt
1 tablespoon vanilla
2 cups grated green tomatoes
3 eggs, beaten
3 cups all purpose flour
1¼ teaspoons baking soda
½ teaspoon baking powder
1 cup chopped nuts
1 cup raisins
½ cup currants

Preheat oven to 350°F.

Add oil, sugar, salt, vanilla, and tomatoes to eggs in large bowl; stir well. Blend in dry ingredients, and stir in nuts, raisins, and currants. Pour into 2 greased 9 × 5 × 3-inch loaf pans. Bake 1 hour.

Jean Kienzlen
Little Falls, New Jersey
Camp-A-Lot Sams

A very quick bread to make with ingredients on hand, Jean's recipe can be baked at a moment's notice. It also can be made ahead of time and reheated.

Serves 8

Jean's Beer Bread

3 cups biscuit mix
2 tablespoons sugar
1 12-ounce can beer, room temperature

Preheat oven to 325°F.

Combine biscuit mix, sugar, and beer. Mix well (batter will be lumpy). Pour into greased 9 × 5 × 3-inch loaf pan and bake 1¼ hours. This is best served warm.

Sally Peterson
Dunning, Nebraska
Loup Valley Sams

A spicy variation of the traditional spoon bread, Sally's version calls for green chilies and sharp cheese. She says it's good with almost any entrée.

Serves 8

Mexican Spoon Bread

| 1 cup yellow cornmeal |
| 1 teaspoon salt |
| ½ teaspoon baking soda |
| 1 cup milk |
| 1 can cream-style corn |
| 2 eggs, beaten |
| 1 7-ounce can whole green chilies, seeds removed |
| 2 cups grated sharp cheddar cheese |

Preheat oven to 450°F.

In medium-size bowl, mix cornmeal, salt, and soda. In another medium bowl, mix milk, corn, and eggs. Blend both mixtures together. Pour ½ into greased 8 × 8-inch baking pan. Spread chilies over mixture and sprinkle ½ of the cheese over chilies. Spoon remaining mixture over cheese and top with remaining cheese. Bake 45 minutes. Cut into squares for serving.

Helen C. Rossell
Barnegat, New Jersey
Garden State Smoke Eaters

For on-the-go RVers, Helen suggests this versatile yeast dough that doesn't require kneading. You'll dazzle your fellow Good Samers at your next chapter potluck when you show up with homemade rolls.

Serves 36

Overnight Refrigerator Rolls

| 2 ¼-ounce packages dry yeast |
| 2½ cups warm water (105°F to 115°F) |
| ¾ cup (1½ sticks) margarine or butter, melted or softened |
| ¾ cup sugar |
| 2 eggs, well beaten |
| 8 cups flour |
| 2½ teaspoons salt |

Soften yeast in warm water. Add shortening, sugar, eggs, 4 cups flour, and salt. After blending, beat 1 minute or until smooth. Stir in remaining flour. Cover tightly and store in refrigerator overnight.

Punch dough down, shape into rolls, and place on greased baking pan or cookie sheet. Cover with clean kitchen towel and let rise in warm area 1 hour.

Preheat oven to 400°F. Bake rolls 15 to 20 minutes. Cool on wire rack.

Hint: For making 12 rolls, punch dough down (after refrigerating overnight), pinch off and use ⅓ of dough, returning remaining dough to refrigerator in covered container. It will keep up to 3 days. Helen also suggests brushing dough with water and eggs beaten together before allowing to rise and after rolls are removed from oven.

Faye Young
Deer Park, Texas
Rovin' Texans

Faye's bread mix is a triple threat: it's easy to store, simple, and versatile—perfect for on-the-road Good Samers.

Makes 12 cups of mix

Faye's Favorite Basic Bread Mix

10 cups flour
⅓ cup baking powder
1½ tablespoons salt
1½ cups shortening (such as Crisco)

Sift dry ingredients twice. Cut in the shortening until it resembles coarse cornmeal. Store this mixture in an airtight covered container at room temperature (in most climates).

Faye's Bread Mix Biscuits. Combine 2 cups of Basic Bread Mix with ⅔ cup milk. Stir well. Knead on lightly floured board until smooth. Roll out to ½-inch thickness. Cut with biscuit cutter. Bake 12 to 15 minutes in lightly greased baking dish at 425°F. Makes about 12 biscuits.

Bread Mix Muffins. Combine 2 cups Basic Bread Mix, ¼ cup sugar, 1 cup milk, and 1 egg. Stir until moistened. Bake in greased muffin tin for 12 to 15 minutes at 425°F. Remove from pans as soon as cooking time is done.

Bread Mix Cake. Mix same ingredients as for muffins. Pour into greased 8-inch-square pan. Brush top with melted butter. Mix together ¼ cup brown sugar, ¼ cup granulated sugar, 1 teaspoon cinnamon, ¼ cup chopped nuts, and 2 tablespoons melted butter. Sprinkle topping mixture over cake. Bake at 375°F for 12 to 15 minutes, until golden brown.

Virginia M. Firebaugh
Fincastle, Virginia
Star Valley Sams

Virginia's not certain where this recipe originated, but she has been preparing it for over 50 years! It's excellent topped with butter, or try it topped with the sauce from fricasseed chicken.

Serves 6

Grandma's Spoon Bread

| 3 eggs, well beaten |
| 1 tablespoon melted shortening |
| ⅔ cup cornmeal |
| ¼ teaspoon baking soda |
| 1 teaspoon salt |
| ¼ cup sugar |
| 2 cups buttermilk |

Preheat oven to 425°F.
Add melted shortening to beaten eggs.
In small bowl, mix cornmeal, soda, salt, and sugar together. Add to egg mixture along with buttermilk. Mix well.
Bake 45 minutes in buttered 1½-quart baking dish or loaf pan. Serve hot.

Honorable Mention
Vieno M. Bradshaw
Poway, California
Weekend Rollers

Who can resist the aroma of baking bread? This unique flatbread comes from the cold country and would be great offered on a chilly camp-out. This bread is good with soup or salad, or just as a snack.

Serves 10

Finnish Flatbread (Rieska)

| 2 cups all purpose flour |
| ½ cup graham flour |
| 2 teaspoons sugar |
| 1 teaspoon salt |
| 1 heaping teaspoon baking powder |
| ¼ cup (½ stick) butter or margarine, softened |
| 1 cup milk |

Preheat oven and cookie sheet to 375°F. In large bowl, mix flour, graham flour, sugar, salt, and baking powder. Cut in butter with pastry blender. Add enough milk, a little at a time, to make dough soft and pliable. Pat out in a round on board dusted with both types of flour. Place on cookie sheet and bake 35 to 40 minutes. Serve warm.

John J. Lucas
Lake Park, Georgia
Member at Large

Because John disliked prepared pancake mixes, he experimented in his galley and devised this homemade mix that is tasty and produces light pancakes. Eventually he and his wife arrived at a proportional mix that gives them three packets of mix for two people. It's easily stored in an RV without refrigeration and is handy when the urge for pancakes strikes.

Each packet makes 4 medium-size pancakes.

Traveler's Pancake Mix

2 cups all purpose flour
2 tablespoons baking powder
4 tablespoons sugar
½ teaspoon salt

Sift together flour, baking powder, sugar, and salt. Measure 6 tablespoons sifted mixture into three self-sealing plastic bags and seal. Label each bag with the following: 1 egg, 1 tablespoon melted butter, and ½ cup milk. These are the ingredients you will need to prepare pancakes for each packet.

When ready to make, mix egg, butter, and milk thoroughly. Add dry ingredients from packet. Mix just to moisten, allowing some lumps to remain.

Preheat griddle to 400°F. Pour onto griddle and brown on both sides.

The ambition of every good cook must be to make something very good with the fewest possible ingredients.

Urbain Dubois, *Esquire*, June 1975

Beverly K. Tudor
Port Neches, Texas
Member at Large

Beverly's unusual treatment of French bread is so easy. She has served it for years to her sorority group and at church socials. It would be delicious offered with a Mexican-style meal.

Serves 16

Greek-style Bread

½ cup (1 stick) corn oil margarine, melted
½ cup mayonnaise
3 medium green onions, chopped with some of the tops
¾ cup chopped black olives
1 loaf French bread, sliced lengthwise
2 cups shredded Monterey Jack cheese

Combine melted margarine and mayonnaise in small bowl and blend with wire whip. Add onions and olives and stir until well blended.

Spread mixture on both halves of sliced bread. Sprinkle with shredded cheese and wrap each half in foil.

Refrigerate overnight, if possible. Bake at 350°F 20 to 25 minutes. Remove from oven and cut each half into 8 slices. Serve bread hot.

Bread, milk and butter are of venerable antiquity. They taste of the morning of the world.

Leigh Hunt, *The Seer*, c. 1840

Clarence R. Lanier
Van, Texas
Free State Sams

When Grandma made biscuits, it was because she couldn't go to her local supermarket and get them out of a refrigerated display case. Even with that option available to the modern cook, there's still nothing like the flavor and aroma of Clarence's freshly baked biscuits.

Serves 18

Cowboy Pan Biscuits

½ cup milk

2 tablespoons vegetable oil

1 tablespoon vinegar

½ teaspoon onion salt

1½ cups biscuit mix

½ cup cornmeal

2 tablespoons vegetable oil or shortening

In a measuring cup, combine milk, oil, vinegar, and onion salt. In medium bowl, combine biscuit mix and cornmeal. Stir in liquid mixture with fork. Form dough into ball. Turn onto floured board and knead 10 times. Shape into 1½-inch balls. Flatten with palm of hand to ¼-inch thickness. In skillet, melt shortening over medium-low heat. Add biscuits. Cook until lightly browned on both sides and cooked through. Add more shortening to skillet if necessary.

Bread always falls on its buttered side.

Anonymous, English proverb

Sweet Breads

Banana Bread

Dorothy A. Tulley
Cypress, California
Solitaire Sams

Everyone's favorite—banana bread—is simple to prepare in your RV using Dorothy's recipe. Serve with coffee when friends drop by.

Serves 10 to 15

1 cup sugar
½ cup (1 stick) butter, margarine, or shortening
2 large eggs, well beaten
⅛ teaspoon salt
1 teaspoon baking soda
1½ tablespoons sour cream
3 medium to large bananas, mashed
2 cups sifted flour
1 cup chopped walnuts
1 teaspoon vanilla

Preheat oven to 350°F.

Cream sugar and shortening together. Add eggs, salt, soda, and sour cream. Mix well. Add bananas, flour, nuts, and vanilla. Mix again.

Line an 8½ × 4½ × 2½-inch loaf pan with waxed paper. Pour batter into pan and bake 1 hour. Cool before slicing.

Quick Raisin-Nut Treats

Mary A. Bentsen
Orlando, Florida
Citrus Sams

When you're in a time crunch, try Mary's quick sweet rolls. There are only 4 ingredients, so you'll save shopping, preparation, and cleanup time.

Makes 10 rolls

1 8-ounce package refrigerator rolls or biscuits
1 8-ounce package cream cheese, softened
½ cup raisins
½ cup chopped nuts

Preheat oven to 400°F.

Flatten rolls or biscuits with fingers. Mix softened cream cheese with raisins and nuts. Place 1 tablespoonful of filling in the center of each roll. Fold dough up and around filling and seal. Place in ungreased 5 × 9-inch baking pan.

Bake 10 minutes or until golden brown.

Hint: You can mix a little cinnamon and sugar into the cream cheese, or use other fruits instead of raisins to vary these treats.

Art Tellone
Phoenix, Arizona
Member at Large

Your family will think they're in a Scottish bed-and-breakfast inn when they wake up to the aroma of Art's scones being baked. They're a refreshing change from biscuits or toast.

Serves 8

Rodey Scones

2 cups flour
2 tablespoons sugar
3 teaspoons baking powder
½ teaspoon salt
⅓ cup butter or margarine
1 egg, beaten
¾ cup milk
1 teaspoon vanilla

Preheat oven to 425°F.

Sift together dry ingredients. Cream in butter until mixture is the consistency of cornmeal. Add egg, milk, and vanilla. Stir quickly until dry ingredients are moistened, adding a little more milk if necessary. Turn dough onto floured surface and knead gently 15 times. Divide into halves and shape into balls. Flatten each ball until dough is ½ inch thick. Cut into wedges. If desired, glaze with beaten egg yolk. Bake 12 minutes or until scones are golden brown.

Hint: If raisins are desired, plump them in warm water before adding to mixture.

Wallace A. Harton
West Hollywood, California
Member at Large

This wonderful sweet bread evolved after several experimental tries. Wallace originally decided to add chocolate chips to plain zucchini bread. Later he added cocoa, since he's such a great chocolate fan. The bread is very versatile and well worth the preparation time.

Makes 1 loaf (10-12 slices)

Chocolate Chip Zucchini Bread

¾ cup vegetable oil

¾ cup sugar

2 large eggs, room temperature

1 pound fresh zucchini, ends trimmed, unpeeled, and finely shredded

1¾ cups all purpose flour, sifted

1 rounded teaspoon baking soda

1 rounded teaspoon cinnamon

¼ teaspoon nutmeg

1½ teaspoons baking powder

3 rounded tablespoons cocoa

6 ounces semisweet chocolate chip morsels, coarsely chopped

½ cup chopped nuts (optional)

Preheat oven to 325°F. Grease a 9 × 5-inch loaf pan.

In large bowl, stir together the oil and sugar until well blended. Beat the eggs and add to oil-sugar mixture, stirring until well blended. Squeeze the zucchini dry with a paper towel and add to oil mixture.

In a separate bowl, mix together the flour, baking soda, cinnamon, nutmeg, baking powder, and cocoa. Blend well and add to zucchini mixture. Blend well again. Add chocolate chips and mix well. Pour mixture into greased loaf pan and bake 1¼ hours. Test for doneness with knife blade or toothpick. Remove from oven and allow to cool in the pan 10 minutes. Turn out from pan, cool, and refrigerate.

Hint: *This cake can be frozen for future use. If adding nuts, combine with chocolate chips. Bread slices are great served with cream cheese and raspberry jam. Or serve with sliced peaches and vanilla ice cream, topped with chocolate syrup, for a heavenly dessert. For breakfast, lightly toast and spread with strawberry jam.*

Grace Almond
Englewood, Colorado
Member at Large

When Grace's in-laws arrived unexpectedly for an overnight visit, she improvised and came up with this delicious breakfast fare. Accompany with crisp bacon or sausages.

Serves 4

Company's Coming Toast

| 8 tablespoons orange marmalade, or more if desired |
| 8 slices raisin bread |
| 2 eggs, beaten |
| 2 cups milk |
| ½ teaspoon sugar |
| 2 tablespoons (¼ stick) margarine |
| Confectioners sugar for garnish |

Spread marmalade on raisin bread. Put slices together to form sandwiches. Beat eggs, milk, and sugar together in a 1-quart bowl.

Dip sandwiches in milk mixture to coat well on both sides. Melt 1 tablespoon margarine in a 10-inch skillet over medium heat and brown sandwiches on both sides, one or two at a time. Add more margarine as needed. Serve immediately with confectioners sugar sprinkled over top.

Vernon Peters
Alta, Indiana
Boomerang Sams

These delicious rolls can be made before the weekend to take with you. Just wrap in foil and pop into oven to warm. Vernon says they're good cold, too.

Makes 8 to 12

Quick and Easy Sweet Rolls

| 1 18.25-ounce box white cake mix, or yellow if desired |
| 3 ¼-ounce packages yeast, dissolved in ½ cup warm water |
| 5½ cups all purpose flour |
| 2½ cups warm water |
| 2 tablespoons (¼ stick) softened butter, or more if desired |
| 4 teaspoons cinnamon |
| 1 16-ounce can vanilla frosting *or* |
| 2 cups confectioners sugar mixed with just enough milk to make thin glaze |

Preheat oven to 350°F. Grease 2 9×13-inch pans.

Pour cake mix into medium bowl. Add flour, dissolved yeast, and warm water. Work mixture, combining all dry ingredients until smooth. Let rise in warm area until doubled in size.

Roll out ½ the dough on lightly floured board to ¼-inch thickness. Spread softened butter over surface and sprinkle with cinnamon. Roll up jelly roll fashion. Cut roll into ½- to 1-inch pieces and place in greased 9×13-inch pan. Repeat with second half of dough. Allow rolls to rise in warm place until doubled.

Bake 20 to 25 minutes. Allow to cool slightly and frost with canned frosting or glaze mixture while rolls are still warm.

Arlie Lehmann
Salinas, California
Member at Large

Arlie's bran muffins are especially good with scrambled eggs at breakfast time, but they also make a filling mid-afternoon snack. Health-conscious Good Samers will appreciate the nutritional value of the ingredients.

Serves 8

Bran Muffins

1 cup bran
1 cup unbleached flour
1½ tablespoons fructose or 2 tablespoons sugar
½ teaspoon baking soda
½ teaspoon salt
⅔ cup buttermilk
1 egg
2 tablespoons vegetable oil

Preheat oven to 425°F.

In medium bowl, combine and mix dry ingredients. Pour buttermilk into 2-cup measuring cup. Add egg and mix until well blended. Add oil and mix again until oil is blended with other ingredients. Add liquid to dry mixture; blend well. Spoon into muffin pan coated with nonstick baking spray. Bake 15 minutes or until lightly browned.

Kissing don't last, cookery do.

George Meredith

Olive B. Hutchison
Leduc, Alberta, Canada
Member at Large

Don't throw out that banana that looks a bit too ripe for eating! Instead, turn to Olive's recipe for bran date loaf and give the family an unexpected treat.

Serves 24

Bran Date Loaf

1 large banana, mashed
2 eggs
⅔ cup brown sugar
¾ cup all bran cereal
¼ cup molasses
⅓ cup butter or margarine, softened
1 cup flour
2 teaspoons baking powder
1 teaspoon mace
1 teaspoon nutmeg
½ cup orange peel
1 cup chopped dates
⅔ cup chopped walnuts

Preheat oven to 375°F.

In medium bowl, beat banana, eggs, and brown sugar. Stir in cereal; let soften. Stir in molasses and butter. Add dry ingredients and mix together. Stir in orange peel, dates, and walnuts. Pour into greased 9 × 5 × 3-inch loaf pan. Bake 1 hour. Loaf will be done when toothpick inserted in center comes out clean.

Hint: Olive likes to butter slices of this loaf for a snack. The bread also keeps well.

Cookery, n.: a household art and practice of making unpalatable that which was already indigestible.

Ambrose Bierce, *The Devil's Dictionary,* 1911

Side Dishes

Potato

Bubble and Squeak

Ruby M. Kidd
Paradise, California
Paradise Roaming Rockers

Ruby's mother gave her this recipe years ago. The recipe is a well-known English dish; the name comes from the sound that it emits as it is cooking.

Serves 4

1 cup mashed or chopped cooked potatoes
1 cup cooked chopped cabbage
2 to 3 tablespoons bacon drippings
Salt and pepper to taste

Mix the cooked potatoes and cabbage together in a bowl. Heat bacon drippings in a 10- or 12-inch skillet. When drippings are hot, add potatoes and cabbage mixture. Season with salt and pepper. Heat the mixture thoroughly, then allow to brown on bottom, adding more drippings if necessary. When well browned, turn out onto serving plate, browned side up. Serve immediately.

Hint: Ruby prefers mashed potatoes, and since she uses leftovers, the amount of potatoes and cabbage can vary according to the amount you have on hand. Other variations of this recipe call for leftover meat to be added to mixture and for browning on both sides before turning out onto plate.

Campground Potatoes

Faye Young
Deer Park, Texas
Rovin' Texans

Faye suggests using a good old-fashioned cast iron skillet to prepare these potatoes. They can be made either in the RV galley or over an open campfire.

Serves 5 to 6

¼ cup bacon drippings or vegetable oil
4 to 6 cups thinly sliced raw potatoes
1 to 2 medium onions, thinly sliced
1 teaspoon salt
¼ teaspoon black pepper
1 teaspoon chopped parsley (optional)

Heat bacon drippings or oil in skillet over low heat. Add potatoes, onions, salt, pepper, and parsley, if desired. Cover and cook about 15 minutes. Stir gently, cover again, and cook until potatoes are tender. Remove cover to allow potatoes to brown, about 5 minutes longer.

Hint: Faye says that the potatoes can be left unpeeled before slicing.

Hash Brown Casserole

Helene Anderson
Paradise, California
Roaming Rockers Sams

Helene's creamy hash brown potato casserole is topped with a crunchy crust. It's a wonderful accompaniment to almost any meal and makes a popular potluck contribution as well.

Serves 8

| 1 cup grated cheddar cheese |
| 1 cup grated Monterey Jack cheese |
| 2 cups sour cream |
| 1 10¾-ounce can cream of chicken soup |
| 3 green onions, finely chopped |
| 1 2-pound bag frozen hash brown potatoes |
| 1½ cups crushed cornflakes |
| 6 tablespoons (¾ stick) butter or margarine, melted |

Preheat oven to 350°F.

In large bowl, mix together the cheeses, sour cream, soup, and onions. Add potatoes and mix well. Place into a 9 × 12-inch baking dish.

Mix cornflakes and melted butter together and sprinkle over top of potato mixture. Bake 1 hour.

Hint: Substitute frozen potatoes O'Brien for a slightly different version.

What I say is that, if a man really likes potatoes, he must be a pretty decent sort of fellow.

A. A. Milne, *Not That It Matters*

Elizabeth Holt
Bella Vista, Arkansas
Member at Large

This hearty dish has been in Elizabeth's family for years. So simple to prepare and serve, it's ideal for potlucks and the RV life-style.

Serves 8 to 10

Johanna's Creamy Vegetable Potatoes

5 cups cooked diced potatoes *or*
1 16-ounce can small whole potatoes
1 15-ounce can baby onions
1 10-ounce package frozen peas or lima beans, defrosted
3 slices American cheese, cut into ¼-inch strips
1 10¾-ounce can cream of celery soup
1 3-ounce package cream cheese
½ cup milk

Preheat oven to 350°F.

Combine vegetables and ½ of the American cheese. In a separate bowl, mix soup, cream cheese, and milk together. Heat the soup-cream cheese-milk mixture over low heat, stirring constantly until well blended. Add heated mixture to vegetables. Turn into a buttered 2½-quart casserole or 8 × 11-inch pan. Arrange remaining cheese strips over top and bake about 45 minutes, or until vegetables are tender.

Hint: This dish can be prepared up to a day before cooking. Be sure to cover and refrigerate.

Betty Condit
Grants Pass, Oregon
River Roosters Sams

A terrific way of serving leftover mashed potatoes, Betty's delicious, economical pie has its derivation from the English shepherd's, or cottage, pie.

Serves 4

Peasant Pie

2 tablespoons butter, margarine, or bacon drippings
3 medium onions, thinly sliced
3 medium carrots, thinly sliced and cooked
3 to 4 cups seasoned mashed potatoes
1 cup shredded Monterey Jack cheese

Preheat oven to 350° F.

Sauté onions in butter, margarine, or bacon drippings. (Betty prefers the latter.) When golden brown, remove from cooking oil and set aside. Brown cooked carrots in remaining drippings, adding a little more oil if necessary.

Layer onions, carrots, mashed potatoes, and cheese in a casserole or (preferably) a deep-dish pie plate, making certain to top vegetables with potatoes and cheese. Bake for 30 minutes.

Hint: Leftover meats can be added for a more substantial main-course dish. Amounts may vary according to the leftovers on hand.

Potato Puff

Darlene Claywell
Lilburn, Georgia
Friendly Sams

Darlene doesn't throw her leftover mashed potatoes away either. Instead she concocts this delicious soufflélike casserole to serve alongside roast beef or other main dish entrées.

Serves 4 to 6

3 tablespoons butter, melted
2 cups cold mashed potatoes
2 eggs
1 cup evaporated milk
Salt and pepper to taste

Preheat oven to 325°F.

In a large bowl, beat melted butter into mashed potatoes until smooth and creamy.

In a small bowl, beat eggs until they are a light lemon color. Add eggs to potato mixture, along with evaporated milk, and beat until smooth and even-colored. Add salt and pepper to taste.

Butter a 1-quart casserole dish. Pour mixture into dish and bake until light brown, about 50 to 60 minutes. Serve immediately.

Rice

Jane Lenius
Stuttgart, Arkansas
Mallard Sams

Versatile enough to serve as a side dish or main course, Jane's tasty chicken and rice combination would also be great for a potluck course.

Serves 8

Chicken-Rice Casserole

2 cooked chicken breasts, cut into bite-size pieces

1 cup cooked celery, diced

¼ cup cooked green pepper, minced

¼ cup cooked onion, minced

1 2-ounce jar pimientos

2 cups cooked rice

1 10¾-ounce can cream of mushroom soup

1 tablespoon lemon juice

¾ cup mayonnaise (do not use salad dressing)

½ cup crushed cornflakes

½ cup slivered almonds

Mix all ingredients together, except cornflakes and almonds, and put into 9 × 13-inch baking dish. Refrigerate overnight, if possible. When ready to bake, preheat oven to 300°F and top dish with cornflake crumbs and almonds. Bake about 45 minutes.

Shirley Jairell
Laramie, Wyoming
Gem City Sams

Shirley serves this zesty rice dish with meat, fish, and poultry, as well as with more traditional Mexican entrées. It's so easy because it can be made and cooked in the same casserole dish.

Serves 4

Green Chili Rice

2 cups cooked rice

1 cup sour cream

1 cup shredded cheddar cheese

1 4-ounce can diced green chilies

½ cup (1 stick) margarine, melted

Preheat oven to 350° F.

Combine all ingredients in a 2-quart casserole. Bake for 1 hour, covered.

Vivian's Fried Rice

Vivian Vickery
Sandusky, Ohio
Vacationland Sams

The first time Vivian tasted fried rice at a Chinese restaurant, she was determined to duplicate the recipe at home. The result is borrowed from the Oriental original, but different . . . and delicious.

Serves 10

½ pound ground beef, mixed with 1 teaspoon salt and ¼ teaspoon pepper
½ cup chopped onion
1 11-ounce can fried rice (Vivian prefers La Choy) *or* 1 6¼-ounce box stir-fry rice
1 14-ounce can bean sprouts, drained
1 4-ounce can mushrooms, drained and sliced
1 8-ounce can water chestnuts, drained and sliced
¾ teaspoon salt
¼ teaspoon pepper
2 eggs
1 tablespoon milk
Soy sauce to taste

While vegetables are draining, brown ground beef and onion in a 12-inch skillet. Add fried rice, drained vegetables, ½ teaspoon salt, and pepper. Mix well and heat thoroughly on medium heat, stirring occasionally.

As vegetable mixture heats, beat the eggs, milk, and ¼ teaspoon salt together. Pour into buttered 6-inch skillet and scramble lightly. Mix in other ingredients just before serving. Serve with soy sauce.

Hint: Instead of ground beef try pork, chicken, or shrimp. Other ingredients can include green pepper, green onion, snow peas, or sugar peas. These should be added when browning the beef so that they can cook slightly.

Marjorie M. Straughan
Spokane, Washington
Member at Large

Margie's pilaf had its beginnings in the Middle and Far East, but microwave cooking has made the preparation extremely simple—and good.

Serves 4

Margie's Rice Pilaf

1 10½-ounce can beef broth or chicken broth
1 10½-ounce can water
1 tablespoon butter or margarine
⅓ cup diced celery
⅓ cup chopped green pepper
⅓ cup chopped onion
¼ cup sliced mushrooms (optional)
Pepper to taste
1 cup long grain white rice

Combine soup, water, butter, vegetables, and pepper in a 2-quart microwave-safe casserole. Cover and microwave 4 to 8 minutes on high (depending on the wattage of your oven) until mixture boils. Remove dish from oven, add rice, cover, and microwave 15 to 17 minutes on medium-low (60% power). Remove from oven and allow to stand 10 minutes.

Hint: Perfect for low- or no-fat diets.

A meal without rice is like a pretty girl with only one eye.

Anonymous, Chinese proverb

Vegetable

Joan Cole
Holt, Michigan
Mid Mitten Mobiles

Joan's nutritious, tasty vegetable dish garnered a prize at the Michigan State Cook-off. Because it's so easy to prepare, RVers will make it again and again.

Serves 6 to 8

Baked Broccoli with Cheese

| 3 cups fresh broccoli florets |
| 1 cup shredded Swiss cheese |
| 3 eggs, hard-boiled and chopped |
| 1 10¾-ounce can cream of celery soup |
| ½ cup milk |
| 1 6-ounce can French-fried onions |

Arrange broccoli in a $9 \times 12 \times 2$-inch greased baking dish. Sprinkle cheese, chopped egg, and ½ of the onions over top.

Mix soup and milk together and pour over broccoli. Bake 45 minutes. Remove from oven and sprinkle remaining onions over dish. Bake 5 minutes longer.

Etta Mlinar
Joplin, Montana
Milk River Sams

These piquant beets are devilishly good and round out a dinner menu with flair. Etta adds honey and mustard to her unique recipe.

Serves 4

Deviled Beets

| 2 cups diced beets, fresh* or canned |
| 3 tablespoons margarine |
| 2 tablespoons prepared mustard |
| 2 tablespoons honey |
| 1 teaspoon Worcestershire sauce |

Mix beets and other ingredients in saucepan, and heat over medium heat. Do not boil. Serve warm.

*To prepare fresh beets, wash 2 medium-size beets and cut off tops, leaving 1 inch of stem attached. Cover with water and boil until tender. Drain and peel before dicing.

Crystal Meyer
Marathon, Iowa
Stormy Water Rollers

Crystal's sweetened carrot dish
would be a nice accompaniment to
baked ham or turkey. RVers who
travel the countryside may be
fortunate enough to choose their
apples at a local orchard—there's
nothing better than freshly
picked fruit.

Serves 8

Baked Carrots and Apples

5 cups sliced carrots, partially cooked
5 cups sliced apples
½ cup flour
⅓ cup granulated sugar
½ cup brown sugar
1 cup undiluted frozen orange juice, defrosted
4 tablespoons (½ stick) margarine

Preheat oven to 350°F.
Layer carrots and apples in a 2-quart baking dish. Mix next 5 ingredients together and pour over carrot-apple layers. Bake 1 hour or until apples are done. Allow dish to cool slightly before serving.

Velma Wischnesky
Sedona, Arizona
Sedona Sams

Velma's family bean recipe can be
doubled for potluck dinners or a
large crowd. It can also be prepared
ahead of time (at least 2 days) and
refrigerated until ready to bake.

Serves 4

Beefy Baked Beans

6 ounces lean bacon
1 medium onion, chopped
¾ pound lean ground beef
⅓ cup firmly packed brown sugar
1 11¼-ounce can tomato soup
1 15-ounce can baked beans (Velma prefers B&M)

Preheat oven to 350°F. (375°F in high altitude).
Fry bacon until crisp, drain all but 2 tablespoons drippings, and set aside in a greased 2-quart casserole dish.
Sauté onion until translucent in remaining drippings. Add ground beef and brown well. Drain excess grease from skillet. Add cooked bacon, brown sugar, tomato soup, and baked beans. Mix well. Pour mixture into casserole and bake 1 hour.

Bob McCulloch
Mandan, North Dakota
Member at Large

When Bob's children were young, he would make up batches of this hearty bean dish and freeze them in 2-pound margarine containers to take on camping trips. "All that had to be done," says Bob, "was to thaw, heat, and Wowla—a hot dish to stick to any cowboy's ribs . . . and mighty tasty, too."

Serves 8 to 10

Cowboy Beans

2 pounds lean ground beef
2 cups barbecue sauce (prepared or homemade)
1 medium Spanish onion, diced
½ teaspoon garlic salt
½ teaspoon whole celery seed
2 teaspoons prepared mustard
¼ cup dark molasses
1 16-ounce can pork and beans
1 15¼-ounce can dark red kidney beans
1 15-ounce can pinto or navy beans
1 8-ounce jar mushrooms

In a large Dutch oven, brown ground beef. Drain off fat. Add barbecue sauce, onion, salt, celery seed, mustard, molasses, beans, and mushrooms to ground beef. Stir well. Bring to boil, then reduce heat and simmer 1 hour. Serve hot, or cool and freeze for later use.

Hint: This dish will turn out as well when cooked in a microwave oven. Place mixture in microwave container and cook 20 minutes on low power. Beans can also be served as a main course.

If pale beans bubble for you in a red earthenware pot, you can often decline the dinners of sumptuous hosts.

Martial, *Epigrams*, c. 80

Charlene Downer
Salem, Oregon
Member at Large

Try serving these beans at your next barbecue. Guests will come back for seconds! Charlene adds a dash of brandy to enhance the flavor.

Serves 6 to 8

Patio Baked Beans

| ⅓ cup firmly packed brown sugar |
| 1 teaspoon instant coffee granules |
| ½ cup water |
| ½ teaspoon salt |
| 1 teaspoon vinegar |
| 1 teaspoon dry mustard |
| 1 large yellow onion, thinly sliced |
| 2 20-ounce cans baked beans (Charlene prefers B&M) |
| ¼ cup brandy or Cognac |
| 4 slices bacon, cut into 4-inch pieces |

Preheat oven to 350°F.

Mix together brown sugar, coffee, water, salt, vinegar, and mustard in saucepan. Cook over low heat for 5 minutes.

Arrange alternate layers of onion slices and beans in a 2-quart baking dish. Pour hot sugar mixture over and bake 45 minutes, covered.

Add brandy or Cognac, and place bacon pieces on top. Bake uncovered 30 minutes longer.

Anne P. Snyder
Wayne, New Jersey
Camp-A-Lot Sams

Anne fondly remembers this dish from her childhood. When she asked for the recipe, her mother replied, "I don't use recipes." So Anne experimented and found these portions to be right.

Serves 4

Cabbage and Bows

| 1 teaspoon salt |
| 3 cups (¾ pound) chopped cabbage |
| 2 tablespoons olive oil or bacon drippings |
| 1 12-ounce package pasta bows, cooked |

Salt cabbage and stir-fry in oil or drippings until crisp-tender. Add pasta bows and fry until bows are crisp. Serve immediately.

Hint: Add a little cottage cheese and mix well for a variation.

Rose Tunno
New Port Richey, Florida
Sampipers

Rose's baked corn borrows from the traditional Indian pudding and corn pudding versions. She started serving this several years ago, and it has become a most-requested item at covered-dish dinners.

Serves 10

Baked Corn Pudding

Corn Pudding

1 8¾-ounce can cream-style corn

1 7-ounce can corn niblets, drained

3 eggs

2 tablespoons flour

1 cup cold milk

1 teaspoon baking powder

Topping

½ cup water

2 tablespoons flour

½ cup (1 stick) margarine

½ cup brown sugar

For corn pudding: Preheat oven to 325°F. Combine all ingredients and beat together with a wire whisk until mixture is completely blended. Pour into a 9×12-inch baking dish. Bake 45 minutes, or until knife inserted in center comes out clean.

For topping: Mix all ingredients together and place in saucepan. Boil on high heat for 1 minute (do not allow to burn). Pour over corn pudding and serve.

There are many ways to love a vegetable. The most sensible way is to love it well-treated. Then you can eat it with the comfortable knowledge that you will be a better man for it, in your spirit and your body too. . . .

M. F. K. Fisher, *How to Cook a Wolf*, 1951

Raymond Fox
Tampa, Florida
Good Sam Sand Dollars

Raymond's easy-to-fix sweet potatoes
can be served with ham or poultry.
Try it at your next holiday
get-together.

Serves 4

One-Pan Candied Sweet Potatoes

1 16-ounce can sweet potatoes

¼ cup pancake syrup (Raymond prefers
Mrs. Butterworth's)

¼ cup light brown sugar

4 tablespoons butter

Place sweet potatoes in skillet. Add syrup, sugar, and butter. Simmer on low heat for 10 minutes, turning potatoes occasionally. Serve immediately.

Estelle M. Pein
Staten Island, New York
Staten Island
Good Sam Adventurers

Estelle's three-bean dish doubles as
either a vegetable or salad. It's
super-easy to make and store and is
best if marinated overnight.

Tangy Triple Treat

1 medium onion, minced

1 16-ounce can kidney beans, drained

1 16-ounce can cut green beans, drained

1 16-ounce can yellow (wax) beans, drained

¼ cup red wine vinegar

¼ cup apple cider vinegar

½ cup vegetable oil

½ cup sugar

½ teaspoon dried basil

½ teaspoon dried tarragon

½ teaspoon dry mustard

1 tablespoon parsley flakes

In large bowl, mix onion and three types of beans together. In jar or blender, combine remaining ingredients; shake well or blend. Pour over beans; chill.

Anita L. Unterbrink
Magnolia, New Jersey
Sandpipers

Anita's easy side dish can accompany turkey on Thanksgiving or almost any other entrée during the year. Peas, frozen or canned, can be substituted for the green beans.

Serves 8

Green Bean Casserole

2 9-ounce packages frozen French-cut green beans, slightly cooked
1 9-ounce package frozen onion rings, prepared according to package directions
3 to 4 celery stalks, finely chopped
2 10¾-ounce cans cream of mushroom soup
1 10¾-ounce can water
¼ cup bread crumbs

Preheat oven to 350°F.

In large casserole dish, alternately layer beans, onion rings, and celery, ending with onion rings on top. Mix soup and water together and pour over casserole mixture. Top with bread crumbs. Bake about 30 minutes or until mixture bubbles. Serve hot.

Hint: For an extra-special touch, serve in puff pastry shells. Bake shells according to directions on package, then fill with bean or pea mixture that has been heated in a saucepan on the range; top each with onion ring, and serve.

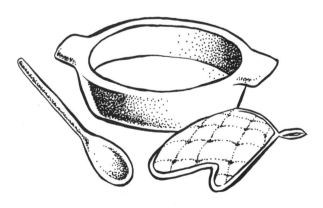

There will be no beans in the Almost Perfect State.

Don Marquis, *The Almost Perfect State*

Joan McKay
Naples, Florida
Naples Smilin' Sams

Fall vegetables and fruit—
rutabagas and apples, in this case—
are sweetened and spiced in Joan's
flavorful vegetable side dish.
Rutabagas, also called yellow
turnips or swedes, were introduced
to our country by the English and
have never tasted better than they
do in this combination.

Serves 6 to 10

Harvest Moon Vegetables

1 to 1½ pounds rutabagas
½ cup raisins
¼ cup water chestnuts, thinly sliced
1 large apple, chopped
½ teaspoon allspice
¼ cup brown sugar
1 cup miniature marshmallows

Preheat oven to 350°F.

Peel rutabagas and dice or slice. (Rutabagas are often coated with wax before being sent to market, so be sure to remove before peeling.) Cook until tender in saucepan with just enough water to cover, about 30 minutes.

Remove from heat, drain, and cool slightly. Mash or process until smooth. Fold in raisins, water chestnuts, apple, allspice, and sugar. Pour into greased 2-quart baking dish. Top with marshmallows and bake ½ hour to heat through.

An accident happened to my brother Jim
When somebody threw a tomato at him.
Tomatoes are juicy and don't hurt the skin.
But this one was specially packed in a tin.

Anonymous

Virginia S. Cummings
Deming, New Mexico
Border Chaparrals

Side dishes don't need to be ho-hum additions to a meal. Try this savory entrée and watch it disappear at your next potluck supper.

Serves 4 to 6

Zippy Zucchini Casserole

1 large zucchini (1 to 1½ pounds), peeled and cubed
1 10¾-ounce can golden mushroom soup
¾ cup grated cheddar cheese
1 egg
2 tablespoons mayonnaise
1 tablespoon chopped onion
Cracker crumbs
Butter or margarine

Cook zucchini until tender; drain. In medium bowl, mix soup, cheese, egg, mayonnaise, and onion together; add drained zucchini. Put mixture into casserole bowl, top with cracker crumbs, and dot with butter. Bake at 350°F for 30 minutes.

Hint: Eggplant or summer squash may be used in place of zucchini. At higher elevations, cooking time may need to be increased. Add some pimiento or crumbled bacon, if desired.

Dorothy Partain
Joshua Tree, California
Joshua Jacks

The ubiquitous zucchini makes another appearance in Dorothy's nutritious, high-protein dish. She uses a nonstick skillet to avoid using oil or grease.

Serves 4

Zucchini Supreme

1 medium onion, chopped
2 medium zucchini, unpeeled and grated
2 eggs, beaten
¾ cup grated cheddar cheese
Salt and pepper to taste

In 12-inch skillet sauté onion over medium heat, about 5 minutes. Add grated zucchini. Cover and steam for 5 minutes. Lower heat to simmer. Add eggs and cheese and cook until custard sets. Serve immediately.

Onion Pie

Lucille Moore
Crossett, Arkansas
Big Pines Sams

Similar to a quiche in texture, Lucille's pie is a novel way of serving onions as a side dish. This would make an outstanding addition to a company dinner, or as a main course for a luncheon.

Serves 8

2 teaspoons butter or margarine
1 cup thinly sliced onions
1 unbaked 9-inch pie shell
3 eggs, slightly beaten
1½ teaspoons flour
2 teaspoons dry mustard
½ cup mayonnaise
1 cup cream or half and half, scalded

Preheat oven to 350°F.

Sauté onions in butter until just tender. Spread over unbaked pastry shell.

In medium bowl, combine remaining ingredients into warmed cream. Mix well and pour over onions. Bake about 40 minutes. Remove from oven and allow to stand 10 minutes before serving.

Minted Carrots and Onions

Nadie Gehrs
Palm Coast, Florida
Member at Large

Nadie adds mint to give a subtle flavor and aroma to an old favorite.

Serves 4

2 tablespoons butter or margarine
2 medium yellow onions, thinly sliced
6 medium carrots, sliced into ¼-inch pieces
1 teaspoon sugar
½ to 1 teaspoon crushed dried mint leaves, or fresh, if available
Salt to taste, optional

Melt butter in a 2-quart saucepan over medium heat. Add onions and cook until transparent. Add carrots, sugar, mint, and salt, if desired. Simmer about 35 minutes, until tender.

Leslie A. Ackerman
Toledo, Ohio
Good Sam Loafers

Leslie's flavorful dish, rich in iron and other nutrients, was a standout at her chapter potluck. Try it at your next get-together.

Serves 8 to 10

Spinach 'n Stuffing Soufflé

¾ cup (1½ sticks) butter or margarine
2 10-ounce packages frozen chopped spinach, cooked according to package directions
1 medium onion, chopped and cooked
4 eggs, beaten
1 6-ounce box prepared chicken-flavor stuffing mix (Leslie prefers Stove Top)
½ cup grated Parmesan cheese

Preheat oven to 350°F.

Melt butter or margarine in small skillet or microwave oven.

In large bowl, mix together melted butter, spinach, onion, and eggs.

Prepare stuffing mix according to directions on package. Add to spinach mixture. Place in greased 9×13-inch baking dish. Sprinkle grated Parmesan over top. Bake 15 minutes. Serve hot.

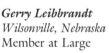

Gerry Leibbrandt
Wilsonville, Nebraska
Member at Large

Gerry's sauerkraut recipe can be prepared in advance either in a microwave or conventional oven and reheated just in time for that Good Sam potluck dinner. It makes a hearty and filling side dish.

Serves 4

Sauerkraut Bake

1 16-ounce can sauerkraut
1 14½-ounce can stewed tomatoes
⅔ cup sugar
¼ cup diced onion
7 slices bacon, fried and crumbled
2 tablespoons rice

Preheat oven to 350°F.

Drain and rinse sauerkraut. In 2-quart casserole dish, mix sauerkraut and all other ingredients. Bake 1¼ hours. If using microwave oven, cook at full power for ½ hour, stirring once or twice.

Pat Ramsey
Butler, Kentucky
Good Sam Angels

Crookneck, or summer squash, should be selected for their small size—the smaller, the more tender they will be. Particularly abundant in early spring, they can be cut, blanched, and frozen for use in winter. Pat tells us that her chapter, the Good Sam Angels, has indoor camp-ins during the winter, and she and her friends enjoy summer squash all year.

Serves 4

Crookneck Squash Casserole

3 to 4 small yellow crookneck squash
3 tablespoons butter
Pinch of salt
12 saltine crackers, crushed
4 slices American or cheddar cheese, cut in 1/4-inch strips
1/2 cup Parmesan cheese
1 1/2 cups milk

Preheat oven to 350°F.

Slice squash across or into quarters or sixths lengthwise. Do not peel. Drop into small amount of boiling water in saucepan and steam-cook, covered, just until tender; drain.

In small buttered casserole dish, layer squash, butter, and salt, if desired. Add 1/2 of the crushed crackers and 1/2 of the cheese. Repeat layers and top off with Parmesan cheese. Pour milk over top and bake until brown on top, 20 to 30 minutes. Serve hot.

Richard Ferolito
Pleasant Valley, New York
Mohawk Majestics

Richard recommends serving these delicious mushrooms, laced with vermouth, with steak. Good Samers everywhere should love the taste!

Serves 2 to 4

Mushrooms alla Ricardo

1/4 cup (1/2 stick) butter or margarine
2 cloves garlic, finely chopped
1 8-ounce can mushrooms, drained and sliced *or*
12 ounces fresh mushrooms, thinly sliced and soaked in water for 2 minutes
Salt and pepper to taste
1/2 cup sweet vermouth
Pinch of flour, for thickening

In an 8-inch skillet melt butter and sauté garlic over medium heat until golden brown. Add mushrooms, salt, and pepper, and cook 1 minute. Add vermouth, reduce heat, and simmer for about 15 minutes, until the juice begins to thicken and reduce. Add flour if needed to thicken. Serve immediately.

Mama Manin's Squash Patties

Jean Westbrook
Hialeah Gardens, Florida
Member at Large

Jean was given this delicious recipe by a "sweet Italian lady who has since passed away." During the depression this woman, needing to feed her large family with what she had on hand, inventively came up with these patties. Jean tells us that everyone who has ever tasted them has loved them—even die-hard squash haters.

Serves 6

2 pounds yellow crookneck squash
¼ cup chopped onion
3 eggs
½ teaspoon garlic salt
¼ cup grated Parmesan cheese
¾ cup self-rising flour
¼ cup vegetable oil

Boil squash until tender. Drain and place in large bowl. Add onion, eggs, garlic salt, and cheese. Mash all ingredients together until most of the lumps are gone.

Slowly beat in the flour with a fork. You should have a mixture the consistency of pancake batter.

Heat oil in 12-inch skillet. Drop batter by large tablespoons into hot oil and fry until golden brown on one side. Turn over and fry other side until brown. Turn out onto plate lined with paper towel and serve hot. Patties also can be kept warm in a 200°F oven until serving time or reheated the next day.

Hint: *Zucchini can be substituted for the squash. Top with pat of butter and sprinkle with Parmesan cheese.*

Shirley Patterson
Blue Springs, Missouri
Member at Large

Shirley's unusual treatment of
the common cauliflower may
make vegetable lovers out of the
most stubborn.

Serves 4 to 6

Fried Cauliflower

½ cup flour

½ cup yellow cornmeal

1 egg, beaten

Salt to taste

Milk to thicken batter

1 small head of cauliflower, washed and
broken into small florets

Combine flour, cornmeal, egg, and salt. Add enough milk to make a thick batter, a little at a time.

Dip pieces of cauliflower into batter and fry in deep fat until golden brown on both sides, approximately 380°F to 420°F in electric fryer. Drain on paper towels and salt while still hot. Serve vegetables immediately.

Cauliflower is nothing but cabbage with a college education.

Mark Twain

Entrées

Beef

Della Wootan
Tucson, Arizona
Catalina Sams
Second Chance Sams

Della tells us that these enchiladas are a hit with all ages. The recipe is especially good for RVing because nearly all of the ingredients are canned, and it's so filling that little else but a salad is needed to make a complete meal.

Serves 8 to 16

Beef Enchiladas Supreme

| 1 20-ounce can enchilada sauce |
| 1 8-ounce can tomato sauce |
| 1 4-ounce can diced green chilies |
| 1 7½-ounce can taco sauce |
| 2 12-ounce cans roast beef with gravy |
| 8 medium flour tortillas |
| 16 ounces longhorn cheese, grated |
| 2 cups shredded lettuce |

Preheat oven to 350°F.

In a medium bowl, combine enchilada sauce, tomato sauce, green chilies, and taco sauce. Put roast beef and gravy in another medium bowl; shred beef with fork. Add 6 tablespoons of sauce mixture into meat mixture and stir.

Spread 4 rounded tablespoons of enchilada-tomato sauce over bottom of 9 × 12-inch baking pan. Dip tortillas, one at a time, in sauce, and spread 2 rounded tablespoons of meat mixture in middle of each tortilla after it is dipped. Roll and place in baking pan. Spread rest of enchilada-tomato sauce over top of rolled enchiladas. Cover with foil and bake 40 minutes.

Remove from oven and cover enchiladas with cheese. Return to oven, uncovered, for 10 minutes or until cheese melts. Just before serving, garnish each enchilada with lettuce.

Hint: For easier cleanup, coat baking pan and shiny side of foil with nonstick cooking spray.

C. G. "Huck" and Marie Mickey
Lompoc, California
Central Coast Sams

Huck and Marie came up with a winner at the Nevada State Samboree Cook-off when they prepared this delicious entrée for the judges. It makes a wonderful company dish or a perfect one-dish meal with leftovers for a small family.

Serves 6 to 8

Beef and Cheese Enchiladas

2 large onions, finely chopped
¼ cup vegetable oil
2 pounds lean ground beef
Salt and pepper to taste
1 20-ounce can medium-hot enchilada sauce
2 8-ounce cans tomato sauce
2½ pounds cheddar cheese, grated
12 medium flour tortillas

Preheat oven to 350°F.

Saute onions in oil until soft. Add ground beef, salt, and pepper, and cook until meat is browned. Remove from heat.

In large saucepan, heat enchilada and tomato sauces. Add ½ pound of the cheese and stir into sauces until melted.

Spread 6 tablespoons of the sauce over the bottom of a 9 × 13-inch baking pan. Dip tortillas into remaining sauce, one at a time, and lay in pan. Place 2 tablespoons ground beef and 2 tablespoons of remaining grated cheese into each tortilla and roll up. Arrange in baking pan. Pour remaining sauce over top and add remaining cheese. Bake 25 to 30 minutes or until cheese bubbles.

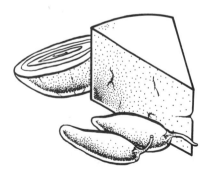

George Fairfield
Bangor, Maine
Four Winds

For more than 30 years, Maine State Director George Fairfield has been whipping up this palate pleaser on open campfires, in his rig, and even at home. People usually are lined up with their plates before the sauce has fully simmered, but George says the longer the flavors blend, the better the results.

Serves 10

Dynamite Fixin's

Sauce

¼ cup vegetable oil

4 medium green peppers, diced

2 medium onions, chopped

½ bunch celery, diced

1 clove garlic, crushed

2 14½-ounce cans tomatoes

2 10½-ounce cans tomato soup

1 6-ounce can tomato paste

3 cups water

1 tablespoon crushed red pepper

Meatballs

1½ pounds lean ground beef

8 soda crackers, finely crushed

1 large egg, beaten

1 small onion, finely chopped

1 clove garlic, finely chopped

1 teaspoon ground cloves

½ teaspoon crushed red pepper

10 hot dog rolls

Salt and pepper to taste

For sauce: Heat oil in 12-inch skillet over medium heat. Sauté vegetables, covered, until tender. Add garlic.

In a 6-quart pan, combine tomatoes, tomato soup, tomato paste, water, crushed red pepper, and sautéed vegetables. Simmer over low heat.

For meatballs: In large mixing bowl, combine all ingredients and mix until blended. Shape into 2-inch meatballs. Brown in pan used for sautéeing vegetables. Add to sauce in pan and continue to simmer over low heat for at least two hours.

Place meatballs on hot dog rolls and pour some of the sauce over. Season with salt and pepper as desired. Serve immediately. This can be refrigerated or frozen for later use.

Third Prize

Della Wootan
Tucson, Arizona
Catalina Sams
Second Chance Sams

Della's recipe was awarded third prize in the International Cook-off. Smelling the aroma as it bakes is the next best thing to being in Italy. The sauce can be made in advance and frozen to be used when the urge comes along to have a really great meal.

Serves 10 to 12

Eggplant Parmigiana

3 pounds ground beef
2 tablespoons dried onion
3 teaspoons salt
1 32-ounce jar spaghetti sauce (Della prefers Ragu)
2 4-ounce cans mushrooms (stems and pieces)
¾ teaspoon sweet basil
¾ teaspoon oregano
1 large eggplant
1 pound mozzarella cheese, grated

Preheat oven to 400°F.

In large pan, cook ground beef with onions and salt; do not allow meat to brown. Drain off excess grease. Add spaghetti sauce, mushrooms, basil, and oregano; simmer 45 minutes.

To prepare eggplant, peel and cut lengthwise into eight slices; each slice should be about ¼ inch thick. Coat 9 × 12-inch baking pan with nonstick baking spray.

Arrange eggplant slices in baking pan; pour sauce over slices and bake 45 minutes. Remove from oven and sprinkle with cheese. Return to oven for 10 minutes; do not allow cheese to brown.

Vivian Vickery
Sandusky, Ohio
Vacationland Sams

Vivian got tired of seeing youngsters picking the kidney beans out of her homemade chili, but she doesn't think chili is really chili without beans. She decided it was time to do a little experimenting and switched to pork and beans. It was popular with the young set as well as adults, and Vivian can continue to make chili for family outings.

Serves 4 to 6

Kids' Chili

1 pound ground beef
½ cup chopped onion
1 quart tomato juice
3 tablespoons catsup
1 21-ounce can pork and beans
½ teaspoon chili powder
Salt and pepper to taste

In a 12-inch skillet, brown ground beef and onion. While this is browning, combine remaining ingredients in 2-quart saucepan. Add meat and onions; cover and simmer 1 hour. Serve with crackers or chips.

Helen Geiger
Zanesville, Ohio
Seneca Sams

You don't have to wreck a ship or your RV to enjoy this one-dish meal that has been handed down in Helen's family. She isn't sure where the name of the recipe originated.

Serves 4

Shipwreck

1 pound ground beef
1 onion, sliced
4 potatoes, sliced
1 15¼-ounce can kidney beans
1 10¾-ounce can tomato soup, undiluted
½ teaspoon salt
¼ teaspoon pepper

Preheat oven to 350°F.
Layer ingredients in casserole in order given. Cover and bake 1½ hours. Remove cover and bake additional 15 minutes.

Catherine Klinger
White Marsh, Maryland
Pleasure Seekers

Catherine got this recipe from her mother-in-law more than 30 years ago and finds it ideal for camping because in just a half-hour you can call the family in for dinner.

Serves 6

Fast and Easy Mac

3 quarts water, salted with 1 teaspoon salt
2 cups elbow or small shell macaroni
1½ pounds ground beef
1 medium onion, diced
½ teaspoon salt
⅛ teaspoon black pepper
1 15-ounce can tomato sauce

In large pan, bring water to boil. Add macaroni and cook until tender; drain and rinse.

While macaroni is cooking, sauté ground beef and onion over medium heat; add salt and pepper. Cook until onion is transparent. Add tomato sauce and cover; simmer over low heat. Add drained macaroni to meat mixture; toss thoroughly. Cover and simmer for 5 minutes. Remove cover and continue to simmer until excess juice is gone, being careful not to burn.

Hint: *If using an electric skillet, sauté meat and onion at 380°F, and simmer mixture at 315°F.*

It matters not how simple the food—
a chop, steak, or a plain boiled or roast
joint, but let it be of good quality and
properly cooked, and every one who
partakes of it will enjoy it.

Alexis Soyer, *The Modern Housewife,* 1851

William A. Williams
Tampa, Florida
Good Sam Sand Dollars

William gave us detailed information on shopping for the ingredients for his recipe: When you get off freight train, find the nearest supermarket—make the butcher mad so he will throw some meat at you; grab it, and run. Then locate dumpster and pick out your vegetables—make it early, so the sun hasn't had time to wilt them. Take fixings back to camp and prepare stew.

Serves 4 to 6

Hobo Stew

1 pound beef, cubed
2 to 3 tablespoons vegetable oil (enough to brown meat)
2 medium onions, chopped
1 14½-ounce can tomatoes
1 teaspoon salt
⅛ teaspoon pepper
1 12-ounce can of beer
1 16-ounce package frozen mixed stew vegetables, thawed

Brown meat in heated oil; add onions.

Put mixture into 3-quart slow-cooker and add tomatoes, salt, and pepper. Cook 3 hours on high setting.

Add beer and vegetables. Continue cooking for 1 hour on low heat.

Hint: Fresh vegetables can be used, as well. Find any combination to your liking.

Honorable Mention

Elizabeth Cook
Greenwood, South Carolina
Good Sams of Faluda Valley

One day when Elizabeth was searching in her RV refrigerator to see what she could find for dinner that evening, she started putting a variety of ingredients in a frying pan. Her children asked her what she was cooking, and her reply was, "stuff." The name stuck and so did the recipe; it was a finalist in the International Cook-off. It's a great one-dish meal for busy RV cooks.

Serves 6

"Stuff"

1 pound lean ground beef
2 medium potatoes, diced
¼ head cabbage, coarsely chopped
2 carrots, coarsely chopped
1 medium onion, coarsely chopped
1 10¾-ounce can cream of chicken or cream of mushroom soup
6 to 8 slices American cheese

Place ground beef in 11-inch stove-top or electric skillet, pressing to cover bottom of pan. Spread vegetables over meat. Pour soup over mixture; place cheese slices on top. Add salt and pepper to taste. Cover skillet. Start with medium-high heat (325°F); when mixture starts to steam, turn to low heat and cook 20 to 25 minutes. Serve immediately.

Sweet and Sour Meatballs

Bernice A. Johnson
Missoula, Montana
Garden City Sams

The tantalizing aroma of Bernice's one-dish meal works better than a dinner bell when it comes to getting Good Samers to the potluck table.

Serves 6 to 8

1½ pounds ground beef
½ teaspoon salt
¼ teaspoon pepper
1 egg, beaten
¼ cup flour
2 tablespoons vegetable oil
2 green peppers, cut into strips
¼ cup water
1 14-ounce jar or 1 2⅛-ounce package sweet and sour sauce mix
1 8¼-ounce can pineapple chunks, drained
1 9-ounce jar maraschino cherries, drained
3 cups cooked rice

Mix ground beef, salt, and pepper; shape into 1-inch balls. Dip each meatball into egg and then flour; brown in oil. Leaving meatballs in skillet, drain off excess grease. Add green peppers and water; simmer 4 minutes. Add sweet and sour sauce (following directions on package, if mix is used). Stir in pineapple and cherries. Cook until all ingredients are hot. Serve with rice.

Joyce Outland
Worland, Wyoming
Cloud Peak Sams

Joyce's entrée is a versatile family dish. For a crowd, just increase the amounts. It's also good for RVing because dehydrated vegetables can be substituted for frozen or fresh ones. What's even better, it can be prepared using just one large skillet, saving on cleanup chores (see optional method).

Serves 6

Creamy Potato-Hamburger Delight

1 tablespoon butter or margarine
1 small green pepper, diced
2 small onions, diced
1½ pounds ground beef
½ teaspoon garlic salt (optional)
Pepper to taste
¼ cup catsup
¼ cup barbecue sauce
1 20-ounce package frozen hash brown potatoes
1 8-ounce carton sour cream
1 10¾-ounce can cream of chicken soup
1 cup grated cheese (American preferred, but other varieties may be used)

Preheat oven to 350°F. In a 10-inch skillet, sauté green pepper and ½ of the onion in butter over medium heat until onion is transluscent. Add ground beef, garlic salt, pepper, catsup, and barbecue sauce. Cook until meat is lightly browned. Pour off excess grease. Divide meat mixture into two portions, and place at each end of 9 × 13-inch baking pan.

Place potatoes into center area of pan. Sauté remaining onion over medium heat until transluscent; sprinkle over potatoes. (Potatoes can be sautéed with onion before placing in baking pan, if desired.)

Combine sour cream and chicken soup; pour over potatoes. Bake 45 minutes. Sprinkle grated cheese over potatoes and return to oven until cheese is melted.

Optional Method: Use larger skillet. After meat mixture is cooked, push it to sides of skillet and cook potato mixture in middle; simmer over low heat until done.

Honorable Mention

Eileen Kuehl
Strawberry Point, Iowa
Backbone Country Sams

Enjoy the tantalizing aroma while Eileen's economical company entrée is baking. Next day, the leftovers make great sandwiches.

Serves 8

Zesty Italian Meat Loaf

| 1½ pounds ground beef |
| 1 egg, beaten |
| ¾ cup cracker crumbs |
| ½ cup chopped onion |
| 1 teaspoon salt |
| 1 cup tomato sauce |
| ½ teaspoon oregano |
| ¼ teaspoon pepper |
| 2 cups grated mozzarella cheese |

Preheat oven to 350°F.

Mix ground beef, egg, cracker crumbs, onion, salt, and ⅓ cup tomato sauce. Add oregano and pepper. On waxed paper, shape into 10 × 12-inch rectangle. Sprinkle with mozzarella cheese. Roll up and press ends to seal. Place in loaf pan and bake 1 hour.

Remove from oven and pour remaining tomato sauce over top of meat loaf. Return to oven and bake 15 minutes longer. Slice and serve immediately.

Plain food and plainly cooked and not too much of it.

Auguste Escoffier, quoted in *Wine and Food,* 1935

First Prize

Ricardina Bentekovics
Parsippany, New Jersey
Member at Large

Ricardina took first place in Good Sam's International Cook-off for her marinated steak that is delicious as well as nutritious. Judges rated it high on flavor and low in calories— a winning combination in today's health-conscious society.

Serves 4

Trim and Slim Flank Steak

1½ pounds flank steak
1 clove garlic
⅓ cup soy sauce
⅓ cup Worcestershire sauce
⅓ cup red wine
8 to 12 ounces fresh mushrooms, sliced
1 tablespoon butter or margarine

With sharp knife, score steak on the diagonal on both sides, making cuts in both directions to form diamond pattern. Rub garlic on both sides. Place meat in shallow pan. Mix next three ingredients and pour over meat; marinate at least ½ hour, turning after 15 minutes.

While meat is marinating, sauté mushrooms in butter or margarine. Heat barbecue or broiler to very high temperature.

Remove steak from marinade and reserve liquid. Grill 4 to 5 minutes on each side; it will cook very rapidly. Remove from heat and place on platter; slice in thin strips against grain and cover with mushrooms. Serve immediately with warmed marinade.

Hint: One teaspoon garlic may be substituted for clove of garlic, but do not use garlic salt. Marinade can be used with other cuts of meat.

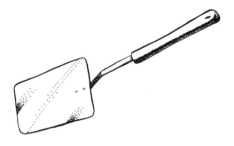

A man seldom thinks with more earnestness of anything than he does of his dinner.

Dr. Samuel Johnson

Marie E. Lavigne
Magnolia, New Jersey
Sandpipers

Marie's delicious dish is a real crowd pleaser and is a great one-pan dinner for a crowd. It also can be prepared ahead and frozen in smaller amounts for family meals.

Serves 8 to 10

Veal Marengo

½ cup vegetable oil

4 pounds veal, cut into 1-inch cubes

1 cup chopped onion

1 cup chopped celery

½ cup chopped green pepper

1 cup dry white wine

2 8-ounce cans tomato sauce

⅛ teaspoon garlic powder

2 bay leaves

1 teaspoon oregano

½ teaspoon rosemary

1½ teaspoons salt

½ teaspoon pepper

1 teaspoon parsley flakes

2 tablespoons flour

2 4-ounce cans sliced mushrooms

1 14½-ounce can stewed tomatoes

Heat oil in 6-quart Dutch oven. Add veal and sauté; remove pieces as they brown.

In same pot, cook onion, celery, and green pepper about 5 minutes, until golden. Stir in ½ of the wine, tomato sauce, seasonings, and veal.

Bring to a boil, then reduce heat and simmer for about 1½ hours until veal is tender. Remove bay leaves.

About 20 minutes before veal is done, combine remaining wine with flour, mushrooms, and stewed tomatoes. Stir into veal mixture. Continue to cook until sauce is slightly thickened and veal is done.

Hint: *Marie says this is fantastic served over hot, buttered noodles.*

Poultry

Lucille E. Hallen
Palo Alto, California
Camino Cavaliers

Lucille decided to improve on her cookbook turkey loaf when she prepared it for a potluck camp-out dinner. One of her innovations is the addition of the hot and mild Italian sausage, lending a zip to the mild flavor of turkey.

Serves 8

My Favorite Turkey Loaf

Turkey Loaf

½ pound mild Italian sausage

¼ pound hot Italian sausage

1¾ pounds ground raw turkey

¾ cup milk

2 eggs

½ cup chopped onion

½ teaspoon salt

½ teaspoon sage

½ teaspoon poultry seasoning

2 tablespoons Worcestershire sauce

1 tablespoon prepared horseradish

¾ cup quick cooking oatmeal, uncooked

Topping

3 tablespoons brown sugar

½ cup catsup

2 teaspoons mustard

For turkey loaf: Preheat oven to 350°F. Remove casings from sausage. Mix sausage and turkey together. Add remaining ingredients and mix until well blended. Lightly pack into 7½ × 11½-inch loaf pan.
For topping: Mix all ingredients together and spread over loaf. Bake 50 to 60 minutes.

Marion Weiman
Turin, New York
Member at Large

Marion's chow mein is so versatile that it can be made with chicken, beef, pork, or ground beef. Even canned meats work well.

Serves 4

Versatile Chow Mein

2 tablespoons cooking oil
2 to 3 stalks celery, diced
2 medium onions, cut in half from crown to root and sliced thin
1 14-ounce can chow mein vegetables, drained
1 cup diced cooked chicken (more if desired)
2 cups chicken consommé or bouillon
Soy sauce to taste
2 to 3 tablespoons cornstarch softened in small amount of water
1 3-ounce can chow mein noodles

Heat oil in skillet. Lightly cook celery and onions; add vegetables, chicken, consommé and soy sauce. Simmer 10 minutes. Thicken with cornstarch. Serve over noodles.

Hint: *For a complete meal, serve with steamed white rice and a pot of hot tea. Serve orange wedges for dessert.*

Donna M. Williams
Lakeland, Florida
The Rowdy Rovers

Donna's entree calls for the surprising addition of cola. It's easy to prepare, especially when camping.

Serves 4

Cola Chicken

1 whole chicken, cut into parts
½ cup catsup
½ cup barbecue sauce, homemade or prepared
1 cup cola

Arrange chicken pieces in large skillet and pour catsup, barbecue sauce, and cola over. Cook over low heat until chicken is tender.

Richard Gee
Paramus, New Jersey
Camp-a-Lot Sams

Tortilla chips and green chilies give Richard's savory casserole a taste of Mexico. Microwaving makes it fast and easy. Serve with a tossed salad.

Serves 6 to 8

Aztec Chicken Casserole

4 whole chicken breasts
¼ cup water
1 10¾-ounce can cream of mushroom soup
1 10¾-ounce can cream of chicken soup
1 4-ounce jar sliced mushrooms, drained
1 large bag plain tortilla chips, crushed
2 7-ounce cans chopped green chilies
1 cup diced onion
1 pound grated cheddar cheese
Salt and pepper to taste

Place chicken breasts in covered 4-quart casserole dish (glass or microwave-safe). Add ¼ cup water. Microwave on high 13 to 18 minutes. Allow to stand 5 to 10 minutes. Remove chicken from bones and cut into bite-size pieces.

Combine soups, mushrooms, and chicken pieces.

Place a layer of tortilla chips (½ of crushed mixture) in a 9 × 13-inch glass baking dish. Layer soup and chicken mixture, chilies, onion, and cheese. Season with salt and pepper. Sprinkle rest of chips over casserole and microwave covered at 50% power 15 to 20 minutes. Let stand for 5 minutes before serving.

. . . fowls are to the kitchen what canvas is to the painter.

Jean-Anthelme Brillat-Savarin
La Physiologie du goût, 1825

Virginia Lakes
Clifton, New Jersey
Fun-N-Nonsense

Virginia's chicken entrée is attractive when served on a bed of rice and garnished with orange slices and parsley. It's great for those special-occasion meals.

Serves 6

Orange Garlic Chicken

3 whole boneless chicken breasts, split in half
Salt and pepper to taste
1 cup chicken broth (can be homemade, canned, or bouillon)
1 teaspoon minced garlic
½ cup orange marmalade
¼ cup white wine

Preheat oven to 350°F. Pound chicken breasts to flatten, and sprinkle with salt and pepper. Place in baking pan in a single layer.

Mix together broth and garlic; pour over chicken. Cover pan with foil and bake 45 minutes or until tender. Pour off most of broth.

While chicken is cooking, combine orange marmalade with wine. Spoon over cooked chicken and return to oven. Bake uncovered in 400°F oven 15 minutes, basting with sauce frequently to give chicken a tasty glaze.

Denise McGuire
Elizabeth, New Jersey
Rolling Rovers

Denise promises fast food for a busy evening. If you use a disposable pan and utensils and paper plates, there's no washing up. Not even a can opener is needed! Serve with whole cherry tomatoes and celery stalks. Pass catsup or duck sauce for dipping.

Serves 4 to 6

Absolutely-No-Washing-up-Setting up-First-Night Dinner

1 20-ounce package frozen French fries
1 18-ounce package frozen chicken nuggets
Catsup, duck sauce or white vinegar and salt for dipping

Preheat oven to 450°F. Spread potatoes over bottom of rectangular disposable pan. Bake 5 minutes.

Remove pan and place chicken nuggets over potatoes. Bake 10 minutes longer. Serve from pan with choice of dipping sauces, or sprinkle with white vinegar and salt.

Lois Horning
New Rockford, North Dakota
Prairie Rose Sams

Lois uses her electric skillet to prepare this tasty entrée, making it easy to take to Good Sam potluck dinners. If dry camped, it can be adapted for a conventional oven.

Serves 8 to 10

RV Skillet Chicken

1 0.8-ounce package vegetable soup mix
(Lois prefers Knorr)

10¾ ounces milk

1 cup uncooked rice

1 10¾-ounce can cream of chicken soup

1 10¾-ounce can cream of celery soup

1 6-ounce can chopped water chestnuts

1 4-ounce can mushrooms

6 chicken breasts

1 2.8-ounce can French-fried onions

In medium bowl, soak soup mix in milk for ½ hour. Add next five ingredients and stir. Pour into electric fry pan. Put chicken breasts on top of mixture and cover. Bake at 225°F for 1 hour or until rice and chicken are tender. Do not bake too quickly. Sprinkle onions on top and bake an additional 5 minutes.

Honorable Mention

Marlene Felton
Victoria, British Columbia, Canada
Van Isle Explorers

Marlene's terrific one-dish meal, a finalist in the International Cook-off, can be prepared for 2 or 20 by just reducing or multiplying the ingredients. It's simple to prepare, leaving the RV chef with more free time to enjoy an outing. Add a salad and watch the food disappear.

Serves 6

RV Chicken Delight

1 cup uncooked long grain rice

1 10¾-ounce can cream of chicken soup

1 can water

3 pounds chicken legs, skin removed

1 1.5-ounce package onion soup mix

Preheat oven to 350°F. Grease bottom and sides of 9 × 13-inch baking pan. Sprinkle rice evenly on bottom of pan. Mix soup and water together; pour over rice. Place chicken on top of rice. Sprinkle onion soup mix evenly over chicken. Cover with foil and bake 1 hour.

Barbara Bailey
Paradise, California
Paradise Roaming Rockers

If your partner's favorite parts of the chicken are the wings, Barbara's tangy chicken recipe will become a much-requested entrée. Serve with fried rice or a stir-fried vegetable.

Serves 4

Saucy Apple Chicken Wings

12 chicken wings
½ cup frozen apple juice concentrate
½ cup water
2 tablespoons soy sauce
1 tablespoon molasses
1 teaspoon ground ginger
½ teaspoon ground cinnamon
½ teaspoon curry powder
⅛ teaspoon cayenne pepper
¼ teaspoon allspice
3 tablespoons sugar

Singe chicken wings if necessary. Cut tips from wings and save for soup stock. Separate each wing at joint. Set aside.

Put apple juice, water, soy sauce, molasses, ginger, cinnamon, curry powder, cayenne pepper, and allspice into a 10- or 12-inch frying pan. Mix well and bring to boil. Arrange wing parts in a single layer in juice mixture. Bring to boil again; cover and lower heat to medium-low. Cook approximately 20 minutes. Stir and turn wings over two or three times during cooking period. Remove cover and raise heat to high. Sprinkle wings with sugar. Cook and stir constantly, about 12 minutes, until sauce boils down, becomes syrupy, and coats the chicken well. Cool slightly and serve immediately.

When I demanded of my friend what viands
  he preferred,
He quoth: "A large cold bottle and a small
  hot bird."

Eugene Field, *The Bottle and the Bird*, 1889

Pork

Cynthia M. Richards
Williams Lake,
*   British Columbia,*
*   Canada*
Cariboo Sams

This delicacy from the Far East is great as a main dish or as an entrée at a potluck supper. No exotic ingredients are needed to prepare the ribs, and they can be fixed at home and reheated just in time for the dinner bell.

Serves 5

Chinese Pork Spareribs

3 to 4 pounds pork spareribs
Salt, pepper, and garlic salt to taste
3 cloves garlic, finely chopped
2 teaspoons ginger root, finely chopped
⅓ cup firmly packed brown sugar
⅓ cup white vinegar
⅓ cup catsup
2 tablespoons soy sauce
1 teaspoon salt
Dash pepper
4 canned peach halves, ½ cup juice reserved

Preheat oven to 450°F. Line 9 × 12-inch baking pan with aluminum foil. Cut ribs into small pieces. Bake fatty side up for 20 minutes. Drain off excess fat. Sprinkle ribs with seasoning to taste.

Place next 9 ingredients, including peach juice, in blender; mix thoroughly. Pour mixture over ribs. Cover with aluminum foil to seal in flavor and juices. Reduce oven heat to 350°F; bake ribs 1½ hours.

Salt is white and pure—there is something holy in salt.

Nathaniel Hawthorne, *American Notebooks*, 1840

Hazel E. Steele
Anchorage, Alaska
Midnite Sun Good Samers

The secret to Hazel's roasted pork entrée is in the delicious marinade. The marinade can be made ahead and frozen, or double portions of the entire recipe can be prepared and half of it frozen for serving later on.

Serves 5 to 6

Chinese-style Barbecued Pork

2 pounds pork loin
Marinade
1 clove garlic, crushed
1 teaspoon salt
⅓ cup Sherry
⅓ cup soy sauce
3 tablespoons honey
⅓ cup maraschino cherry juice (optional)
1 teaspoon grated ginger root
½ teaspoon five spice powder

For marinade: Mix together all ingredients.
For final dish: Pour marinade over pork loin and refrigerate overnight. When ready to roast, preheat oven to 325°F. Bake 1½ to 2 hours on rack set into large roasting pan. Baste with marinade at end of 1 hour and once again before cooking time is done. Cool, slice, and serve with hot mustard and toasted sesame seeds on the side.

Rosemary H. Phillips
Winchester, Virginia
Shenandoah Sams

This versatile entrée can be made with or without potatoes, depending on your taste and desire to trim calories (see optional method). Trimming the fat from the chops also is recommended for the calorie conscious. Side dishes can be enhanced with the gravy from this casserole.

Serves 4

Pork Chops in Celery Sauce

1 10¾-ounce can cream of celery soup
1 10¾-ounce can water
¼ cup flour
4 pork chops
2 tablespoons shortening
Salt and pepper to taste

Dilute the soup with water; stir until smooth. Set aside. Preheat oven to 350°F. Flour chops and brown lightly in shortening in a skillet. Season with salt and pepper. Place chops in 2-quart baking dish; pour celery soup mixture over chops. Cover dish and bake 1 hour or until chops are tender.

Optional Method: Arrange sliced raw potato over chops, then cover with soup mixture (potatoes will cook in same time it takes to cook pork chops).

Frances Harmer
Winnipeg, Manitoba, Canada
Manitoba Goldeyes

Frances likes this meal-on-a-bun because it can be prepared ahead of time and stored in the freezer for a quick meal on the road. It's especially good for hearty young appetites. Who needs to go out for pizza?

Serves 4

Pizza on a Bun

½ pound bacon, cut into small pieces
1 small onion, finely chopped
1 small green pepper, chopped
¼ cup chopped celery
¼ cup chopped broccoli
½ cup grated cheddar cheese
½ 10¾-ounce can golden mushroom soup
½ cup vegetable juice
1 4-ounce can mushrooms (either stems and pieces or whole mushrooms)
½ cup grated mozzarella cheese
4 French rolls

Before leaving home: Fry bacon and onion together until bacon is crisp; drain off excess grease. Add remaining ingredients except mozzarella cheese and French rolls. Simmer mixture until cheddar cheese melts and celery is tender. Freeze in small containers.

To serve: Defrost as much of the vegetable mixture as you need. Preheat broiler to 375°F. Slice French rolls in half. Spread prepared mixture on rolls. Top with mozzarella cheese, and place under broiler until cheese melts. Serve immediately.

Robert C. Faller
Las Cruces, *New Mexico*
Dona Ana Peppers

Pozole (poh-soh-leh) is a hominy stew of Mexican-American origin. Robert's easy version is moderately spicy and would make a delicious meal rounded out with corn bread or warmed tortillas and a salad. Complete the meal with a make-ahead dessert, such as a custard.

Serves 2 to 3

Gringo's Easy Pozole

2 medium pork chops or pork steaks
1 medium yellow onion, diced
1 15-ounce can hominy, golden or yellow
1 15-ounce can peeled tomatoes, chopped into bite-size pieces, liquid reserved
1 4-ounce can peeled green chopped chilies, undrained
½ teaspoon garlic powder
½ teaspoon chili powder
¼ teaspoon cumin (optional)
¼ teaspoon salt
¼ teaspoon pepper

Trim the meat from the bones and dice into ½-inch pieces.
In a lightly greased 3-quart saucepan or large skillet, fry the meat until slightly browned; add onion just before the meat is done. Continue cooking until onions are tender. Add all remaining ingredients, including the juice from the cans. Do not add any additional liquid. Bring to a slow, rolling boil and continue cooking for 15 minutes. Serve hot in soup bowls.

Hint: Accompany stew with an assortment of vegetable relishes and cheeses instead of a salad.

Pepper is small in quantity and great in virtue.

Plato, *Laws,* 360 BC

Florence Niquidet
Williams Lake,
*   British Columbia,*
*   Canada*
Cariboo Sams

Florence was making spareribs for a
Good Sam potluck supper when she
decided to do some experimenting
with prepared spaghetti sauce. She
was pleased with the results, and so
were the lucky ones who got to try
out the dish. She prefers pork
sideribs for this recipe.

Serves 10

Super Spareribs

| 4½ pounds pork spareribs |
| 2 tablespoons butter |
| 1½ cups diced onion |
| 1 cup diced celery |
| 2 32-ounce jars spaghetti sauce (Florence prefers Ragu) |
| 1 4-ounce can sliced mushrooms |
| ½ cup water |
| ¼ cup cider vinegar |
| ¼ teaspoon dry mustard |
| ½ cup brown sugar |
| ¼ teaspoon salt |
| 1 teaspoon Worcestershire sauce |

Preheat oven to 375°F. Cut spareribs into serving pieces; place in Dutch oven. Roast, uncovered, 1 hour or until browned. Extract excess grease with baster.

While spareribs are cooking, prepare barbecue sauce. In 2-quart saucepan, cook onions and celery in butter until tender, stirring frequently. Add remaining ingredients; heat uncovered until sauce bubbles.

After removing grease from spareribs, cover with sauce and continue to bake 1 hour.

Hint: Onions and celery can be cooked in microwave oven for 6 minutes. Spareribs can be made in large quantity and then frozen in meal-size containers.

The art of dining well is no slight art, the pleasure not a slight pleasure.

Michel de Montaigne, *Essays*, 1580–1588

Mary Didreckson
Stockton, California
Hub City Sams

Mary returned from the Azores with this recipe as a souvenir. The combination of wine, cinnamon, and pickling spices give it a delicious sweet-sour taste. Serve with Finnish Flatbread (page 81) for an unusually good dinner.

Serves 8 to 10

Portuguese Pork

1 cup distilled white vinegar
1 cup red wine
1 cup water
¼ cup lemon juice
2 teaspoons salt
2 teaspoons cumin seed
1 teaspoon cinnamon
1 tablespoon pickling spice
4 cloves garlic, crushed
1 teaspoon crushed red pepper
6 pounds pork roast, cut in thick slices (boneless shoulder)

Pour all ingredients except pork in saucepan and heat over medium heat. Pour over pork that has been placed in a glass bowl. Cover and marinate in refrigerator overnight.

When ready to roast, preheat oven to 350°F. Drain all but 2 cups of the marinade from meat. Place pork and reserved marinade in 10 × 16-inch roasting pan. Bake 1 to 1½ hours.

Ruby Kidd
Paradise, California
Paradise Roaming Rockers

Ruby's mother gave her this recipe for the soufflélike dish many years ago. It's classic Scottish-English fare and easy to prepare.

Serves 4

Toad-in-the-Hole

1 pound link pork sausages
½ cup hot pork drippings
1 cup all purpose flour, sifted before measuring
2 eggs
1 cup milk
½ teaspoon salt

Preheat oven to 425°F.

Brown sausages slowly in a 10- to 12-inch skillet; set aside.

Place a 2-quart glass casserole dish in oven with ½ cup of the sausage drippings. (Dish must be preheated before the batter is added.)

Place sifted flour, eggs, milk, and salt in blender and mix until well blended. Arrange sausages in heated dish and pour batter over top. Bake 30 to 40 minutes and serve immediately.

Savory Skillet Sausage

B. Fay Kirlin
Clayton, Delaware
Member at Large

Fay finds this a good weekend take-along. Accompany with a fresh vegetable salad.

Serves 4

2 tablespoons olive oil
1 pound Italian sweet sausage, sliced into 2-inch pieces
1 medium onion, sliced in thin strips
1 large green pepper, sliced in thin strips
Salt and pepper to taste
1 cup water
3 medium potatoes, preboiled and sliced

Heat oil in 12-inch skillet. Add sausage and brown on low heat. Add onion and pepper; season to taste. Add water and simmer, covered, until pepper and onion are soft, adding more water if necessary. Add potatoes. Serve when potatoes are heated.

Hint: For heartier appetites, serve on hot dog buns with spicy mustard.

The way to a man's heart is through his stomach.

Fanny Fern, *Willis Parton*

Fish

Norma W. Hall
Ontario, Oregon
Member at Large

Norma tells us that she first prepared this recipe using a Coleman two-burner gas stove while camping with her family in south-central Alaska and later on fishing trips with their travel trailer, using a gas stove. Her rule is: The person who catches the fish is responsible for cleaning and dressing them.

Serves 4

Trout Norma

4 fresh trout, about 12 to 14 inches, preferably rainbows
2 cups milk, fresh or diluted evaporated
1½ cups pancake flour mix (see page 82)
2 teaspoons salt, or to taste
1 teaspoon pepper, or to taste
Cooking oil to cover fish in skillet
½ pound fresh or canned mushrooms, sliced
1 tablespoon butter or margarine
Lemon wedges
Parsley for garnish

Use skillet only slightly larger than size of fish. Place fish in pan and cover with milk. Soak at least 30 minutes, turning fish several times.

Drain fish and give the milk to the dog, Norma says.

Place pancake flour in large paper or plastic bag. Sprinkle salt and pepper inside fish and place in bag, one at a time. Shake bag carefully to coat fish inside and out with flour.

Heat oil in deep frying pan to moderately hot but not smoking. Place fish in hot oil and fry, turning to brown on both sides. Be careful not to overcook. Drain on paper towels and set aside.

Sauté mushrooms in butter or margarine until cooked through. Serve fish on individual plates, topped with sautéed mushrooms and accompanied by lemon wedges and parsley.

Hint: When preparing fish, clean and scale, remove heads and fins, but leave tails intact. Serve with baked or fried bananas, rice pilaf, and a tomato-avocado salad.

J. Lee Preston
Anchorage, Alaska
Top of the World Sams

Next time you can pick up some
fresh fish, try this unusual recipe, a
first-prize winner in the Alaska
State Samboree Cook-off. It looks as
pretty as it tastes. J. Lee
recommends halibut, but says the
sauce can be used for other fish,
including cod or red snapper.

Serves 8

Mexitex Halibut

2 pounds halibut
1 medium onion, chopped
1 medium green pepper, chopped
2 jalapeño peppers, seeded and chopped
1 cup mayonnaise
½ pound medium cheddar cheese, grated
Salt
Lemon pepper

Preheat oven to 450°F. Cut halibut into serving pieces and arrange in 8 × 12-inch baking dish. In medium bowl, mix onion, green pepper, jalapeño peppers, mayonnaise, and cheese. Spread over halibut. Season to taste. Bake 20 minutes or until fish flakes. Overcooking will make fish tough and dry.

Hint: For a milder flavor, use only half of onion and green pepper and 1 jalapeño pepper.

From the beginning of Time to this day, the sea has been man's magic larder; without plough and without pay there has always been . . . a ready supply of fish for man to catch and woman to cook.

André Simon, *The Concise Encyclopedia of Gastronomy,* 1952

Ron Beek
Winnipeg, Manitoba, Canada
Sunny Sams

Ron's recipe for this classic French dish is superb. Serve these creamy baked scallops with a dry white wine, such as Chardonnay, a crisp salad, and French bread.

Serves 4

Ron's Coquilles St. Jacques

½ cup dry white wine
1 pound fresh sea scallops, or frozen
¼ pound small fresh shrimp
3 tablespoons butter
¼ cup chopped onion
2 tablespoons flour
Dash of white pepper
½ cup milk
½ cup chopped mushrooms
½ cup shredded Swiss cheese
¼ cup buttered bread crumbs

Pour wine over scallops and shrimp in a small saucepan. Heat, covered, over low heat 10 to 15 minutes or until tender, stirring once or twice as needed. Drain liquid and reserve ½ cup. Let scallops stand, covered.

In a medium saucepan, sauté onion in butter until tender. Stir in flour and pepper. Gradually add milk and reserved liquid from seafood, stirring until smooth. Heat mixture 5 to 6 minutes, or until thickened, stirring constantly. Add mushrooms, cheese, scallops, and shrimp.

Spoon mixture into individual buttered ramekins or custard cups and top with buttered bread crumbs. Place under broiler with oven set at 400°F 5 to 8 minutes. Serve immediately.

Fish must swim thrice—once in the water, a second time in the sauce, and a third time in wine in the stomach.

John Ray, *English Proverbs*, 1670

Winifred J. Joos
Eau Claire, Wisconsin
Sawdust City Sams

Winifred's flavorful casserole is nutritious and easy to make. It's a good company meal at home or on the road. In areas of the country where seafood is abundant, this would be particularly economical.

Serves 6 to 8

Wild Rice and Shrimp

1 cup wild rice, uncooked

4 tablespoons butter or margarine

2 teaspoons salt

2 tablespoons chopped green pepper

2 tablespoons chopped onion

2 tablespoons butter or margarine, melted

1 tablespoon lemon juice

¾ teaspoon Worcestershire sauce

1 teaspoon dry mustard

¼ teaspoon pepper

½ cup cubed cheddar cheese

½ pound uncooked shrimp, peeled and deveined

1 10¾-ounce can cream of mushroom soup

Place wild rice in strainer; rinse thoroughly. Soak 1 hour in warm water to cover rice; most of water will be absorbed. Place rice in top of double boiler with 2 cups boiling water, butter or margarine, and salt. Cover and simmer about 2 hours.

When rice is almost done, preheat oven to 375°F. Lightly grease a 1½-quart baking dish. Put cooked rice in dish, add remaining ingredients, and mix. Bake 30 to 35 minutes.

What is literature compared with cooking?
The one is shadow, the other is substance.

E. V. Lucas, *365 Days and One More*

Charles R. Pickett
Hudson, Florida
Active Loafers of Hudson

Charles says fish is good for the heart and this dish is good for the tastebuds. Imitation crab meat is inexpensive and just as tasty as the real thing.

Serves 6

Crab-stuffed Fish

6 fish fillets (grouper, haddock, flounder, or your choice)
3 tablespoons lemon juice
½ cup milk
1 clove garlic
2 tablespoons vegetable oil
1 medium onion, chopped
1 small tomato, finely chopped
½ teaspoon parlsey flakes
Salt and pepper
5 ounces imitation crab meat, chopped
4 ounces processed cheese food spread, cut in small pieces (Charles likes Velveeta)
8 ounces plain yogurt
1 egg yolk
½ cup (1 stick) butter or margarine

Wash fillets, rub with lemon juice, and soak in milk.

Sauté garlic in oil until golden brown; remove. Sauté onion in the same oil until golden brown; add tomato and cook until thickened. Remove from heat and add parsley, salt, and pepper to taste. Add crab meat and ⅓ of the cheese and mix well.

Remove fillets from milk and dry well with paper towels. Salt and pepper, if desired. Place ⅙ of filling on each fillet and roll up, enclosing the filling carefully. Place fish rolls in one layer in a greased glass baking dish.

Mix egg yolk and yogurt. Pour yogurt mixture over fillets. Sprinkle with remaining cheese and dot with margarine.

Bake at 350°F until fish rolls are golden brown and the cheese has melted.

Charles R. Sims
Tampa, Florida
Good Sam Sand Dollars

Golden, white, or gray mullet are best for eating, but catfish, bass, mackerel, or perch may be substituted in Charles's recipe.

Serves 4 to 8

Hush Puppies and Mullet a la Ritz

Hush Puppies

1 large onion, diced

1 16-ounce can tomatoes

1 16-ounce cream-style corn

Salt and pepper to taste

Tabasco sauce to taste

3 cups self-rising cornmeal

1 cup self-rising flour

Mullet

2 to 4 pounds mullet, catfish, or mackerel

1 cup milk

2 eggs

1 cup seasoned flour (salt and pepper added)

1 package crackers (Charles uses Ritz), crushed into fine crumbs

For hush puppies: Combine onion, tomatoes, and corn in large bowl. Mix thoroughly, using hands to mash and combine. Add salt, pepper, and Tabasco.

In another bowl, combine cornmeal and flour. Add just enough of the tomato-corn mixture to make a thick, doughy paste. Use teaspoon to shape hush puppies into rounded ovals. Drop into deep fat fryer and fry until golden brown, about 2 to 3 minutes. They will float to the top and turn themselves over when done. Remove, drain, and serve with mullet.

For mullet: Combine milk and eggs. Roll fish in seasoned flour. Dip into egg-milk mixture and then into cracker crumbs until well coated. Drop fish into deep fat fryer and cook until they float to top, about 1 to 2 minutes. Remove and drain. Serve hot with hush puppies.

Meatless

Hazel Horner
Oxnard, California
Member at Large

It's sometimes hard to come up with ideas for meals for two. Hazel's light and airy soufflé is a delicious suggestion. Add a salad and some fruit, and you have a different and delightful dinner.

Serves 2 to 4

Cheese Soufflé

1 cup grated cheese (your choice)
1 cup soft bread crumbs
1 cup milk
3 eggs, separated
1 tablespoon butter
1/8 teaspoon dry mustard, if desired

Preheat oven to 350°F.

Set aside egg whites. Beat remaining ingredients together in a saucepan, and cook over low heat until the mixture begins to thicken. Remove from heat and cool.

Beat egg whites until stiff; fold into cooled mixture. Pour into buttered 1½-quart baking dish. Bake 25 minutes at 350°F.

Mock Chilies Rellenos

Virginia Monti
Elk Grove, California
Sunrise Sams

Virginia's family loves chilies rellenos, but they are difficult to make, so she's come up with this easier version of a traditional Mexican favorite.

Serves 4 to 6

2 4-ounce cans green roasted chilies
12 ounces grated Monterey Jack cheese
6 ounces grated sharp cheddar cheese
2 eggs
2 tablespoons milk
1 tablespoon flour
1 teaspoon garlic salt

Preheat oven to 375°F.

Cut chilies into strips. Lightly grease an 8-inch square baking pan and layer chilies and cheeses.

Beat eggs, milk, flour, and garlic salt together, and pour over layered ingredients.

Bake about 30 minutes, or until firm.

Hint: These can be cut into small squares and served as an appetizer.

One-Pan Scramble Deluxe

Lou Ann Hand
Exeter, California
Member at Large

This nutritious and easy supper is perfect after a day on the road. Lou Ann says you can't miss if you want to enlarge the recipe for guests.

Serves 2

2 to 3 tablespoons butter
½ to 1 yellow onion, chopped *or*
2 green onions, chopped
½ zucchini, chopped
3 to 4 mushrooms, sliced
3 to 4 eggs
Milk (small amount for desired consistency)
Salt and pepper to taste
Grated Monterey Jack cheese, to taste

In a 10-inch skillet, melt butter. Sauté onions and zucchini very lightly; add mushrooms and sauté quickly.

Whip eggs with milk, and add salt and pepper to taste. Add to vegetables in pan and scramble together. Be careful not to overcook mixture.

Top mixture with cheese; place lid on skillet, with heat turned off, until cheese is melted. Serve immediately.

Hint: Lou Ann likes to use the time waiting for the cheese to melt to prepare toast, or heat rolls in the side of the pan under the lid, and to cut up a juicy melon to go with the meal.

Charlotte Roeller
Clifton, New Jersey
Passaic Valley Drifters

Everybody loves pasta dishes, and here's another you can use with your favorite Italian-style sauce. Charlotte hopes you enjoy it.

Serves 8

Stuffed Shells

1 12-ounce box jumbo pasta shells
16 ounces ricotta cheese
8 ounces mozzarella cheese
½ cup grated Parmesan or Romano cheese
4 eggs
½ teaspoon pepper
1 teaspoon garlic powder
1 tablespoon parsley
Italian sauce

Preheat oven to 350°F.

Boil shells in water for about 10 minutes. Drain and rinse with cold water.

Mix cheeses, eggs, and seasonings together.

Use a teaspoon to stuff the shells with the mixture. Put one layer of stuffed shells into a baking dish and cover with sauce. Continue layering shells and sauce. Bake 1 hour.

Elaine Erickson
Agoura, California
Member at Large

This incredibly easy side dish can be made in one dish at the last minute, if necessary, promises Elaine. It's especially convenient for camping or fulltiming.

Serves 4

Ten-Minute Micro Mac and Cheese

2 tablespoons butter or margarine

1 small onion, chopped

1 tablespoon flour

2 tablespoons powdered milk

¾ cup water

½ pound processed cheese food spread, diced (Elaine likes Velveeta)

¼ teaspoon garlic salt

¼ teaspoon white pepper

2 cups cooked macaroni

In 1-quart covered microwave dish, melt margarine (times will vary with your microwave oven). Add onion and cook until soft, about 1 to 2 minutes on high. Add flour and stir to make a roux. Add all other ingredients except macaroni and microwave 4 minutes or until cheese is melted. Add macaroni, mix well, and cook 1 minute longer or until bubbly.

Hint: This is a great way to use leftover macaroni.

There is an inevitable ritual about serving and eating spaghetti ... eaten as it should be, in varying degrees of longness and a fine uniformity of writhing limpness and buttery richness and accompanying noisy sounds.

M. F. K., Fisher, *An Alphabet for Gourmets*, 1949

Leanna G. Spivey
Chesapeake, Virginia
Sandy City Sams

Leanna's light, flavorful quiche
would be perfect fare for a
summer dinner.

Serves 6 to 8

Vegetable Quiche

6 ounces grated cheese,   **(Leanna likes ½ Colby and ½ Swiss)**
1 tablespoon flour
1 10-inch pie crust (ready-made deep dish, or   **homemade)**
1 cup mixed vegetables, cooked and diced
Cooked, crumbled bacon, ham, or seafood, if desired
6 eggs
1 pint half and half
1½ teaspoons salt
2 tablespoons chopped parsley or dill

Preheat oven to 350°F.

Mix cheese and flour together and sprinkle over pie bottom. Layer vegetables on top of cheese. Add meat or seafood, if desired.

Beat eggs with half and half and seasonings.

Pour mixture into pie shell and bake 1 hour or until puffed and browned.

Hint: Leanna uses a 6- to 8-ounce package of frozen mixed vegetables which have been thawed and drained to make this recipe even easier.

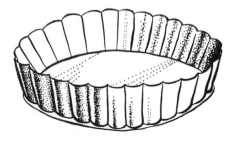

Henriette Shevenell
Jupiter, Florida
Go-Go Angels

Henrie's easy one-dish preparation allows hungry RVers a quick, satisfying meal with plenty of vegetables and cheese for protein.

Serves 4 to 6

Ratatouille Henrie

¼ cup olive oil, butter, or margarine

2 medium onions, chopped

1 medium green pepper, chopped

1 clove garlic, minced, *or*

1 teaspoon garlic powder

Enough chopped fresh vegetables to make 1½ quarts (squash, zucchini, eggplant, cabbage, and carrots) *or*

2 15-ounce cans mixed vegetables, drained, *or*
2 15-ounce packages mixed frozen vegetables

2 8-ounce cans tomato sauce

2 teaspoons basil

2 teaspoons parsley, minced

1 teaspoon marjoram

¼ teaspoon cumin

½ cup cooked rice or macaroni (optional)

1 8-ounce package shredded sharp cheddar cheese

Heat oil or butter in 10-inch skillet. Add onion, green pepper, and garlic. Sauté until onion is soft and translucent. Add vegetables and cook until tender. Add tomato sauce and seasonings and mix well. Stir in rice or macaroni, if desired. Add cheese around sides of vegetables, cover with foil, and continue cooking until cheese has melted, about 5 minutes longer.

The kitchen is a country in which there are always discoveries to be made.

Grimod de la Reynière, *Almanach des Gourmands,* 1804

Outdoor Cooking

Beef

Alvin and Ruth Cote
Victor, Montana
Sapphire Sams

The Cotes's unusual method of cooking beef has been a highlight of the Sapphire Sams' September outings for the past five years. Preparing this meal takes some advance planning and involves every member of the chapter.

Serves 40

Beef in a Pit

22 pounds boneless, rolled bottom round or chuck steak
2 tablespoons liquid smoke
Salt, pepper, onion salt, and garlic salt to taste

You will need the following: ½ cord firewood, aluminum foil, butcher paper, cord, clean burlap or canvas, long piece wire, and wire cutters.

On the day before meat is to be served, dig pit about 5 feet long, 3 feet wide, and 4 feet deep. Pit should be narrower at bottom than top. Pile sand or dirt alongside pit. Line bottom with large, dense river rocks. Build fire in bottom of pit; keep a large fire burning all day, adding wood as needed. There should be at least 16 inches of hot coals in pit.

While fire is burning, season meat. Wrap first in aluminum foil, sealing well, then in butcher paper. Tie with cord to secure.

Soak heavy burlap or canvas in water. If burlap bags are used, do not put meat inside bags; wrap soaked bags around meat. Secure with wire, leaving a piece at least 20 inches long to extend above ground when meat is buried; this serves as a locator.

Put 12 inches dirt on top of hot coals in pit; tramp well. Place wrapped meat on top of dirt and cover with 12 more inches dirt, tramping well again. Make certain meat is completely covered with dirt; you should not see any smoke coming from pit. Be sure locator wire is visible.

Build fire on top of pit and let it burn out. Next day, when ready to serve meat, remove top layer of dirt and remove meat from pit. Remove wire with cutters and unwrap meat. Save cooking juices for barbecue sauce. Slice and serve.

Hint: Take ample wood for fire; pine works well. When removing meat from pit, be very careful not to get burned.

Phyllis Hadley
Ogden, Utah
Northern Utah Golden Spikes

A chuck roast can be just as tasty
and tender as a more expensive cut
of meat when following Phyllis's
directions for cooking it over a
charcoal fire. The secret is in
the marinade.

Serves 6 to 10

Grilled Marinated Roast Beef

1 2 to 3½-pound chuck roast
Marinade
½ cup Burgundy
¼ cup cider vinegar
¼ cup peanut oil
1 onion, chopped
1 celery stalk, chopped
1 tablespoon prepared mustard
1 teaspoon Worcestershire sauce
1 teaspoon rosemary
1 to 2 cloves (½ teaspoon) crushed garlic

For marinade: Blend ingredients 1 minute in blender. Pour over meat. Allow to marinate for 6 hours or overnight.

Cook over very hot coals, turning often. Baste occasionally with marinade. Cook 15 minutes on each side for medium rare.

Hint: The more frequently you turn the roast, the better the juices and flavor will be seared into the meat.

The knightly sirloin, and the noble
baron of beef.

Sir Walter Scott, *Old Mortality,* 1816

Marion Creason
Manchester, Michigan
Member at Large

The juice of the meat permeates the vegetables for a delicious, quickie meal. This was a favorite on family camp-outs when the Creason children were youngsters.

Serves 1

Hamburger and Veggies

1 medium ground beef patty
1/4 large yellow onion, chopped
1 large carrot, cut into 1/4-inch-thick slices
1 medium potato, diced
1/4 teaspoon salt
Dash pepper

Place patty on square of aluminum foil large enough to wrap securely. Add remaining ingredients and seal with foil. Cook over hot coals.

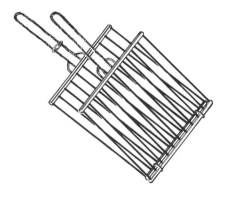

The best of all sauces is hunger engendered by exercise in the open air, and, equally, the best of digestives is pleasant company.

St. Ange

Chicken

Marie E. Houmes
Stone Mountain, Georgia
Carefree Sams

Possibly the most unusual recipe we received was Marie's for preparing chicken. Marie begins her instructions by telling us to walk along a creek and pick up rocks that water flows over, about the size of an adult's hand and flat on the bottom. (We add, be sure the rocks are dense since shale ones may explode when heated.)

Serves 4 to 6

Creek Rock Chicken

---

3 creek rocks, 1 to fit inside the chicken's cavity and 2 small, flatter ones to fit under the chicken wings

---

3 pounds charcoal

½ cup butter or margarine

Salt and pepper to taste

---

1 2½ to 3-pound chicken

Heavy duty foil

Several newspapers

---

1 cardboard box to hold chicken

Wash the creek rocks and allow to dry thoroughly. Light charcoal, and, once the coals are white, place creek rocks over hot coals. Allow rocks to heat until very hot.

While the rocks are heating, coat the chicken with the margarine and season with salt and pepper.

When rocks are quite hot, remove with tongs and (using potholders or mittens) wrap them in the foil.

Place foil-wrapped rocks into chicken—one into the cavity and the flatter ones under each wing. Wrap the chicken and rocks in heavy foil and wrap in several layers of newspaper. The more newspaper the chicken is wrapped in, the better it will cook and retain heat.

Place chicken in cardboard box and set aside. Enjoy a game of horseshoes for 3 to 4 hours. When your game is over, your chicken will be ready.

Everything tastes better outdoors.

Claudia Roden, *Picnic*, 1981

Fish

Barbecued Fish

Richard H. Sharp
New Port Richey, Florida
Active Loafers of Hudson

While the coals are getting hot, Richard cleans and fillets his freshly caught fish and prepares to enjoy that special treat reserved for dedicated fisherfolk.

Serves 8

8 fish fillets
2 cups French-style dressing
3 cups cracker crumbs

Dip fillets in dressing; coat with crumbs. Lay fillets on grill about 4 to 5 inches above coals. Brush with more dressing. Cook 3 minutes on each side; do not overcook.

Hint: Fish fillets are fully cooked when they become flaky. Recipe is good for bluegill, perch, or bass.

Foil-wrapped Fish

Dolores Brown Gilman
Pittsfield, New Hampshire
Member at Large

Forget about washing dishes tonight. Dolores tells us this fish entrée can be cooked in aluminum foil and eaten right out of the package.

Serves 1

1 fish fillet for each serving
1 small yellow onion, diced
1 stalk fresh celery (celery salt can be substituted)
1 small green pepper, diced
Salt and pepper to taste
1 ounce butter or margarine (Dolores suggests low-fat margarine if watching weight or cholesterol)

Lay each fillet on piece of aluminum foil large enough for wrapping fish. Add onion, celery, and green pepper. Sprinkle with salt and pepper. Add margarine. Wrap tightly and bake directly on hot coals or on grill 20 minutes.

Mary E. Brown
Kermit, Texas
Sandhills Good Sams

Mary comes from a fishing family and has been cooking fish fillets for 40 years. Since her family didn't like their fish fried in cornmeal, she found a popular alternative and serves it on camp-outs as well as at home.

Serves 2 to 3

Mary's Fried Fish

1 cup flour
1 pound fish fillets
1 cup milk
1 cup cracker crumbs seasoned with 1 tablespoon salt

Heat fat in deep fryer. Put flour in plastic bag. Drop fillets, one at a time, in bag and shake to coat. Dip each fillet in milk, then coat with cracker crumbs. Place on waxed paper until all fillets are coated. Cook in deep fat until golden brown.

Hint: When back from a fishing trip, prepare fillets for frying and place on cookie sheet covered with waxed paper. Freeze until ready to use; do not thaw before cooking.

Richard C. Farrer
Hayward, California
Member at Large

Whether cooking for special friends or for a cozy dinner for two, Richard's barbecued shrimp is sure to please anyone lucky enough to be around for this flavorful entrée.

Serves 4

Shrimp on the Barby

$\frac{1}{3}$ cup butter or margarine
$\frac{1}{4}$ cup chopped green onion
$\frac{1}{3}$ cup chopped parsley
$\frac{1}{4}$ teaspoon Worcestershire sauce
Drop hot pepper sauce (or more to taste)
Salt to taste
12 (1 pound) raw jumbo shrimp, peeled and deveined
1 cup thinly sliced mushrooms

In double boiler, melt butter. Add next 5 ingredients and stir. Cut 4 squares of foil. Place 3 shrimp on each square. Put $\frac{1}{4}$ prepared seasonings on shrimp; add $\frac{1}{4}$ of the mushrooms. Fold foil tightly. Place each package directly on coals with seam side up. Cook 10 to 15 minutes. Shake package one time during cooking process. Remove from coals. Cut foil at seam with scissors.

Pork

Julia M. Eastman
Cheyenne, Wyoming
Sunbird Good Sams

Julia learned about cream can dinners from her daughter's mother-in-law. She started to experiment with various ingredients and came up with a combination that should be a real crowd pleaser on your next chapter outing.

Serves 30

Cream Can Dinner

25 medium red potatoes, scrubbed
5 heads cabbage, quartered
25 carrots, peeled
15 medium white onions, peeled
20 ears corn
35 small Polish sausage links
1½ pints water

Layer vegetables and sausage in 10-gallon cream or milk can, alternating frequently so sausage flavor reaches all vegetables. Add water. Close lid tightly. Place over small wood fire that has been prepared between 2 8-inch cement blocks, with can resting on blocks. Keep fire burning for 2 hours. After steam comes from can, cook another 15 minutes. Remove can from fire. Remove lid from can and carefully lift out ingredients with long tongs.

Hint: Use fresh vegetables when possible. If corn is not in season, substitute with frozen ears of corn. German sausage may be preferred.

Cooking is like love—it should be entered into with abandon, or not at all.

Harriet van Horne, *Vogue*, 1956

Marie E. Houmes
Stone Mountain, Georgia
Carefree Sams

Marie contributed several unique recipes (see her Creek Rock Chicken, page 155), and her version of baked ham is included, even though you may not have the equipment to prepare it yourself. But if your group is planning a potluck or get-together, it might just be the most unusual entrée you've ever made.

Serves 35 to 40

Pig-in-the-Hole

| 1 20-pound whole cured ham |
| 20 pounds charcoal |
| Charcoal lighter fluid |
| 1 cup brown sugar |
| 1 20-ounce can pineapple rings |
| Several toothpicks |
| Heavy foil wrap |

Dig a hole large enough to hold the entire bag of charcoal. Be sure and mound the dirt up around the edges as you dig; you will use it later.

Empty the bag of charcoal into the hole and light briquets. Let burn until coals are white.

Wrap ham in double foil, using drugstore wrap. When coals are hot and white, move half of hot coals to side. Place wrapped ham on top of remaining bed of coals and replace the coals you set aside over top of ham, making sure to cover ham completely.

Replace soil that was set aside over top of hot coals and down side, covering hole completely.

Enjoy yourself for 5 hours (or 15 minutes per pound). When time is up, remove only as much dirt as you need to get to the ham. Again, set dirt to one side; you will need it. Remove hot coals from top of ham and set aside for use later.

Remove ham and unwrap carefully. Cover with the brown sugar and fasten pineapple rings around ham with toothpicks. Rewrap ham with foil, being careful not to prick foil with toothpicks, and place back into hole. Cover again with coals and then the dirt. Tell everyone the pig will be done in 45 minutes (it will).

A man hath no better thing under the sun than to eat, and to drink, and to be merry.

The Bible, *Ecclesiastes I, 24* 200BC

Gabrielle Sherman
Waynesville, North Carolina
Mountaineer Sams

Gabrielle finds this recipe great for camp-outs because most of the preparation can be done at home. She packages the ribs and sauce before leaving home, and all she has to do is grill them at the campsite.

Serves 6

Rancho Ribs

1 14-ounce bottle catsup
¼ cup water
2 teaspoons dry mustard
½ teaspoon chili powder
1 teaspoon celery salt
½ teaspoon ground cumin
¼ teaspoon ground cloves
2 tablespoons brown sugar
¼ cup vinegar
¼ teaspoon hot pepper sauce
2 tablespoons Worcestershire sauce
1 tablespoon grated onion
6 pounds spareribs

Combine all ingredients except ribs and blend thoroughly. Cover ribs with sauce and marinate in refrigerator 24 hours. Drain ribs, reserving marinade. Grill over hot coals, using marinade to baste during cooking. Turn ribs often.

Hint: Ribs can be cooked in 300°F oven for 1 hour.

Dewey A. Bjork
Aurora, Minnesota
Member at Large

Dewey orders his pork chops from his local meat market and has them cut into 1- to 1¼-inch-thick slices, leaving the flat bone intact. His secret to barbecuing pork chops is to stand them up, resting on the flat bone, while cooking.

Serves 6

Grilled Pork Chops

6 loin pork chops cut 1 to 1¼ inch thick
Seasoned salt, to taste
Pepper, to taste
Soy sauce for glazing
Garlic salt (optional), to taste
Barbecue sauce (optional)

Season chops with salt, pepper, soy sauce, and garlic salt. Lay flat on barbecue grill and sear each side 3 to 5 minutes. Stand chops up on large, flat bone; place cover on barbecue. Cook 20 minutes. Remove cover and brush chops with barbecue sauce. Replace cover and cook 5 minutes.

Vegetables

Phyllis Hadley
Ogden, Utah
Northern Utah Golden Spikes

When you're already preparing your main entrée on the barbecue, don't let that extra grill space go to waste. Give the cleanup crew a break by preparing this great potato recipe to accompany your steaks or burgers.

Serves 6

Cheese Potatoes in Foil

3 large baking potatoes, scrubbed, peeled, and sliced

Salt and pepper to taste

4 slices cooked bacon, crumbled

1 large onion, sliced

½ pound cheddar cheese, cubed

½ cup (1 stick) butter or margarine

Place potato slices on large piece of foil which has been coated with nonstick cooking spray. Sprinkle with salt and pepper. Spread bacon, onion, and cheese over potatoes; dot with butter. Wrap loosely and seal with double fold. Cook over hot charcoal fire 45 minutes or until done, turning frequently.

Hint: If your meal doesn't call for barbecuing, cook potatoes in 350°F oven until tender.

Even an old boot tastes good if it is cooked over charcoal.

Anonymous, Italian proverb

Mary Naverman
Newell, Iowa
Stormy Water Rollers

Several years ago, Mary wanted to prepare a special meal for nursing home residents. She tried this vegetable entrée, and the patients , as well as her family and friends, loved it.

Serves 6 to 8

Vegetable Potpourri

1 5-foot strip heavy aluminum foil
6 medium potatoes, cut into ½-inch slices
3 medium onions, peeled and sliced
8 carrots, cut into 2-inch pieces
½ cup (1 stick) butter or margarine, sliced
Salt and pepper to taste

Prepare foil by folding in half lengthwise, shiny side folded in. Spray well with nonstick baking spray to within 6 inches of each end. Arrange vegetables on foil; add butter, salt, and pepper. Fold ends over two or three times, using "drug store" method of folding. (Leave a little space to allow the steam to expand.)

Place on barbecue grill about 6 inches above white-hot charcoal. Cook 45 minutes to 1 hour, turning every 5 to 10 minutes to avoid burning. Serve hot.

Gordon C. Vath
Stewart, Minnesota
Crow River Sams

Gordon's recipe for sweet corn makes it possible to enjoy the flavor of fresh corn without having to eat it off the cob. It's quick and easy.

Serves 1

Fresh Cut Corn

2 large ears sweet corn, kernels cut off cobs
1 tablespoon water
1 tablespoon butter or margarine
½ teaspoon sugar

Form a cup with a 12 × 12-inch sheet of aluminum foil. Put water in bottom. Add corn and butter; sprinkle with sugar. Close foil to keep heat in. Barbecue for 10 minutes.

There's no sauce in the world like hunger.

Miguel de Cervantes, *Don Quixote*, 1605–1615

Dessert

Marjorie Bedeker
Washington, Indiana
Cherokee Sams

Sitting around a campfire is much more enjoyable when sharing something good to eat. Marjorie sent us her recipe for a sweet treat that's fun to fix and delicious, too.

Serves 8

Mock Angel Food Cake

1 loaf unsliced stale bread; crust removed and cut into 2-inch squares
1 12-ounce can sweetened condensed milk
1 7-ounce package shredded coconut

Dip bread cubes in milk until well covered. Roll in coconut. Place on barbecue fork and roast over fire until lightly browned.

Marinades and Sauces

Shirley McInnis
Durango, Colorado
Member at Large

A camp-out isn't complete without a barbecue. Shirley likes to enhance the flavor of steak by marinating it before it goes on the grill.

Makes 1½ cups

Shirley's Super Marinade

¾ cup red wine
¾ cup vegetable oil
1 1.25-ounce package onion soup mix
½ to ¾ teaspoon thyme
1 clove garlic, finely minced

Combine ingredients in large self-sealing bag. Add steak. Marinate ½ to 2 hours, turning at least once.

Harold Haddock
Denison, Texas
Texoma Sams

When planning a camping trip, Harold makes this sauce four or five days in advance. Although he prefers it with chicken, it is equally good on steaks or pork chops.

Makes 1 cup

Harold's Chicken Sauce

½ cup honey
½ cup catsup
1 tablespoon garlic powder
3 tablespoons hickory-flavored liquid smoke
1 teaspoon seasoned salt
3 teaspoons chopped onion
2 tablespoons water

In a medium saucepan, bring all ingredients to boil. Cover and set aside. When cooled, marinate chicken or steaks in sauce 4 hours or overnight. Brush on meat while cooking on the grill.

DeLoss Starke
Sublette, Kansas
Member at Large

DeLoss uses "fairy-ring" mushrooms for this sauce, but you can use any fresh commerical mushrooms, or even canned, drained button mushrooms.

Enough for 2 large steaks

Yummy Mushroom Steak Sauce

4 to 6 large mushrooms or 12 to 14 fairy-ring mushrooms
8 tablespoons water
4 tablespoons (½ stick) butter or margarine
4 tablespoons chopped onion
2 tablespoons Burgundy
2 beef bouillon cubes, crushed
1 heaping teaspoon flour

Wash and stem mushrooms and slice.

In 1-quart saucepan, combine 4 tablespoons of the water, butter or margarine, onion, wine, and bouillon. Bring to boil over medium heat and simmer, covered, for 5 minutes.

Mix remaining water and flour well and add to simmering mixture. Bring back to a boil and simmer, uncovered, 5 to 6 minutes more, stirring constantly. Serve over steak or roast beef.

Florence L. Kaufman
Columbus, Ohio
Capitol City Sams

Florence makes plenty of this barbecue sauce because it keeps well under refrigeration and adds that special touch to barbecued meats or chicken.

Makes about 1¼ cups

Spicy Sauce

1 cup catsup
¼ cup lemon juice
1 tablespoon soy sauce
2 tablespoons brown sugar
1 tablespoon horseradish mustard
1 tablespoon grated onion
¼ teaspoon hot pepper sauce
1 whole clove garlic
1 teaspoon salt
½ teaspoon pepper
¼ teaspoon thyme
¼ teaspoon cayenne pepper

In a medium saucepan, combine ingredients. Simmer 10 minutes. Remove garlic. Use immediately or cool and refrigerate.

Cook, see all your sauces be sharp
and poynant in the palate, that they may
commend you . . .

Francis Beaumont and John Fletcher

Linda White
Covina, California
Member at Large

Linda's tangy and thick barbecue sauce enhances chicken, ribs, and other cuts of meat. It also can be used for a simple hors d'oeuvre.

Makes about 3 cups

Barbecue Sauce a la Linda

1 14-ounce bottle catsup
1 tablespoon soy sauce
1 teaspoon chili powder
1 teaspoon garlic salt
2 teaspoons prepared mustard
3 tablespoons lemon juice or white vinegar
¾ cup jam or jelly (each flavor provides a different taste; Linda's favorites are plum, grape, and apricot)
2 tablespoons brown sugar
½ cup diced onion (optional)

Combine all ingredients and blend thoroughly. Brush on meat while cooking. Leftover sauce may be stored in refrigerator in covered jar.

Hint: For hors d'oeuvres, cut 1 package wieners into 1-inch pieces. Add to sauce and heat.

Part of the secret of success in life is to eat what you like and let the food fight it out inside.

Mark Twain

Desserts

Cakes and Pastries

Banana Cupcakes Supreme

Peggy Collette
Suncook, New Hampshire
New Hampshire Wanderers

Don't toss out those overripe bananas. Instead, treat the family to freshly baked banana cupcakes. If there are any left over, serve at breakfast.

Serves 12

| 1 cup sugar |
| ½ cup (1 stick) butter or margarine |
| 1 egg, slightly beaten |
| 2 cups flour sifted with 1 teaspoon baking soda and 1 teaspoon salt |
| 3 ripe bananas, mashed |
| 1 teaspoon vanilla |
| 2 tablespoons honey |
| Pinch of cinnamon |

Preheat oven to 350°F. Cream sugar and butter; add egg and mix. Add dry ingredients, bananas, vanilla, and honey; mix well. Pour into a well-greased muffin pan. Bake 30 minutes.

Hint: For variety, add walnuts, bran cereal, or sunflower seeds. This can also be baked in a loaf pan for 50 minutes.

Bring on the dessert. I think I am about to die.

Pierette Brillat-Savarin, last words, 1911

Caroline A. Miller
Eagle River, Alaska
Midnight Sun Good Samers

Caroline took ordinary cake and frosting mixes and whipped up a crunchy creation that is flavorful and easy to make.

Serves 16

Banana Crunch

5 tablespoons butter or margarine
1 cup quick oatmeal
1 9.9-ounce box coconut pecan frosting mix
4 medium bananas, mashed
4 eggs
1 cup milk
1 1.25-pound box yellow cake mix

Preheat oven to 350°F.

In medium pan, melt butter; add oatmeal and frosting mix (do not follow directions on box). Mix until crumbly; set aside.

In large mixer bowl, blend bananas, eggs, and milk. Beat with mixer at medium speed for 1 minute. Add cake mix (do not follow directions on box). Mix until well blended.

Pour alternate layers of frosting mixture and cake mixture into greased bundt pan, starting and ending with frosting. Press last layer down with spoon to moisten. Bake 1 hour. Cool 15 minutes before removing from pan.

Hint: For best results, use very ripe bananas.

Spread the table and the quarrel will end.

Anonymous, Hebrew proverb

Susann Nacke
Louisville, Kentucky
Derbytown Sams

Susann's toffee cake is good for breakfast, brunch, or dessert. The caramel flavor goes well with a steaming cup of coffee or hot chocolate. It was a favorite with Susann's family when she was growing up, and now her own children enjoy it.

Serves 12

Double Toffee Delight

Topping
1½ cups brown sugar
1 tablespoon cinnamon
1 cup chopped pecans

Cake
2 cups self-rising flour
1 cup sugar
1 3½-ounce package instant vanilla pudding mix
1 3½-ounce package instant butterscotch pudding mix
4 eggs
1 cup water
¾ cup vegetable oil

For topping: In small bowl, combine topping ingredients. Mix well, then set aside.

For cake: Preheat oven to 350°F. Grease and flour 9 × 13-inch cake or tube pan. In large bowl, combine all ingredients for cake; beat at medium speed for 2 minutes.

Pour ½ of cake batter into pan; layer with ½ of topping. Spread remaining batter in pan and layer with remaining topping. If using 9 × 13-inch pan, bake 45 minutes; for tube pan, bake 1¼ hours. Cake is done when toothpick inserted in center comes out clean. Cool before removing from pan.

Hint: Since pudding starts to solidify soon after being mixed, make topping mix first; it will be easier to spread cake batter before it sets.

Ethel L. Faller
Las Cruces, New Mexico
Dona Ana Peppers

Ethel's versatile cake recipe can be used over and over again, substituting a different type of fruit or pie filling each time. It's particularly appealing to RVers because the ingredients "travel" well.

Serves 12

Easy Spread Cake

1 20-ounce can crushed pineapple, undrained
1 21-ounce can cherry pie filling
1 1.25-pound box yellow cake mix
¾ cup (1½ sticks) butter or margarine, thinly sliced
¾ cup coarsely chopped pecans or walnuts

Preheat oven to 350°F. Grease 9 × 13 × 2-inch baking pan. Spread crushed pineapple and juice, cherry pie filling, dry yellow cake mix, butter slices, and chopped nuts evenly in pan. Bake 45 to 60 minutes. Cake will be done when bubbly and golden on top. Cool and serve.

Ilene Hamre
Williston, North Dakota
Camino Cavaliers

Ilene's frosted cake is light and fluffy, with just a little tang. Easy to prepare, it can be frozen to serve later.

Serves 20

Tangy Orange-Pineapple Cake

Cake
1 1.25-ounce box lemon or yellow cake mix
1 15-ounce can mandarin oranges, undrained
4 eggs
⅔ cup vegetable oil

Topping
1 15-ounce can crushed pineapple, undrained
1 5¼-ounce package instant vanilla pudding mix
1 8-ounce container whipped topping

For cake: Preheat oven to 350°F. In a large bowl, combine cake mix, oranges, eggs, and oil. Beat well with hand mixer (or use electric mixer). Pour into a 9 × 13-inch baking pan that has been greased and floured. Bake 30 to 35 minutes. Remove from oven and cool on wire rack.
For topping: Combine pineapple in juice and pudding mix; beat until stiff. Add whipped topping and gently fold in. Spread on cooled cake.

Madelene Kellner
Jessup, Maryland
Essex Pandas

This moist and crunchy cake is as pleasing with a hot cup of coffee in the morning as it is with a glass of milk for a bedtime snack. It's good right out of the oven or chilled and served with a dollop of whipped topping or ice cream.

Serves 15

Harvest Cake

4 cups peeled and diced apples
2 cups sugar
2 eggs, beaten
1 cup vegetable oil
1 teaspoon vanilla
3 cups flour
1 teaspoon salt
2 teaspoons baking soda
1 teaspoon cinnamon
1 teaspoon nutmeg
1 cup raisins or chopped walnuts (or ½ cup each)

In medium bowl, coat apples with sugar. Let stand 1 hour. Preheat oven to 350°F. Grease 10-inch tube pan. In large bowl, mix eggs, oil, and vanilla. Add apples and mix well. Mix dry ingredients and add to mixture; batter will be stiff. Add raisins or walnuts. Pour into pan and bake 1 hour.

Hint: When batter gets too stiff for portable electric mixer, finish mixing with wooden spoon or spatula. Cake can be baked in two loaf pans or one 9 × 13-inch baking pan.

Eat, drink, and be merry, for tomorrow ye diet.

Lewis C. Henry, editor, *Toasts for All Occasions*

Patricia M. Cahill
Colorado Springs, Colorado
Member at Large

Patricia first made this rich chocolate cake in 1951 in Bad Kreuznach, Germany, from a German recipe in metric measurements and using block chocolate. She finally reduced it to its present simple form. Moist, but not messy, it's perfect for potlucks, picnics, or a lunch pail.

Serves 12 to 15

Travelin' Gal's Chocolate Cake

1½ cups diced dates

1 teaspoon baking soda

1 cup plus 3 tablespoons hot water

1 cup sugar

1 cup (2 sticks) butter or margarine

2 eggs, beaten

½ teaspoon salt

2 cups flour

1 tablespoon cocoa

1 tablespoon vanilla

1 cup chocolate chips

½ cup chopped nuts

Preheat oven to 350°F. Place dates in small bowl. Sprinkle with baking soda; add hot water. Let stand 5 to 10 minutes to plump dates.

In large mixing bowl, cream sugar and butter or margarine together. Add eggs and beat well. Sift salt, flour, and cocoa together. Add dry ingredients to sugar-butter mixture in small amounts, alternating with date mixture. Add vanilla and mix well. Fold in ½ cup of chocolate chips.

Pour into greased and floured 9 × 13 × 2-inch baking pan. Sprinkle remaining chocolate chips and chopped nuts over top. Bake 40 to 45 minutes, or until toothpick inserted in center comes out clean.

Daisy Ostrander
Naugatuck, Connecticut
Member at Large

*Try serving Daisy's sweet bread
instead of heavy pies and cakes after
a full meal, topped with butter,
cream cheese, peanut butter, or just
plain. It also fits into the RV life-
style because it can be made ahead
of time and frozen.*

Serves 12

Daisy's Dessert Bread

| 4 cups flour |
| 3 tablespoons sugar |
| 1 tablespoon baking powder |
| 1 teaspoon salt (less can be used) |
| 1 teaspoon baking soda |
| 6 tablespoons (¾ stick) butter or margarine, softened |
| 16 ounces glacéed fruit |
| 1½ teaspoons grated lemon peel |
| 2 eggs, beaten |
| 1½ cups sour milk (use ¼ cup vinegar to sour milk) |

Preheat oven to 350°F. Grease and flour 1½-quart round casserole dish.

In large bowl, mix flour, sugar, baking powder, salt, and baking soda. Cut in butter and mix until coarse crumbs form. Stir in glacéed fruit and lemon peel.

Reserve 1 tablespoon beaten egg and set aside. Add remaining eggs and sour milk to dry ingredients. Dough will be sticky.

Turn dough onto well-floured board and knead with floured hands to mix thoroughly. Shape into ball and place in casserole.

With sharp knife, cut x in top of loaf and brush with remaining beaten egg. Bake 1¼ hours or until done. Cool.

Hint: For variety, in place of glacéed fruit use chopped dates, nuts, chocolate chips, or any combination of these items to equal 16 ounces.

Friends are like melons, Shall I tell you why?
To find one good you must a hundred try.

Claude Mermet, 1600

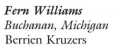

Fern Williams
Buchanan, Michigan
Berrien Kruzers

Fern's wonderful dumplings will be welcomed on a chilly day when they are served still warm from the oven. Use a good baking apple, such as Rome Beauty, and your favorite pie crust recipe.

Serves 6

Grandma's Apple Dumplings

Dumplings
Dough for 2-crust pie
6 medium apples, cored and peeled
6 teaspoons sugar
2 teaspoons cinnamon
2 tablespoons (¼ stick) margarine or butter
Syrup
1 cup sugar
2 cups water
1 teaspoon cinnamon
3 tablespoons butter or margarine

For dumplings: Preheat oven to 375°F. Roll out dough, cut in 6 squares, large enough to cover each apple. Place an apple in center of each square. Fill center of apple with sugar, sprinkle with cinnamon, and top with pat of butter. Bring four corners of dough up and over top of apple. Press lightly to secure. Place in 9×9×2-inch baking dish.

For syrup: Mix all ingredients together in small saucepan and bring to boil. Cook 5 minutes and pour over dumplings.

Bake 15 minutes. Lower heat to 350°F and continue baking 25 minutes or until apples are done. Serve warm; drizzle syrup over apples before serving.

After a good dinner, one can forgive anybody, even one's own relatives.

Oscar Wilde, *A Woman of No Importance*, 1894

Honorable Mention

Mary M. McConnell
Madison, Wisconsin
Yehara Blackhawks

This moist and easy-to-whip-up cake is topped with a whisky glaze. As a bonus, there's no frosting to mess up the RV galley.

Serves 16

Whisky Cake

Cake
1 1.25-pound box yellow cake mix
1 cup milk
4 eggs
1 3½-ounce package instant vanilla pudding mix
½ cup vegetable oil
¼ cup whisky
1 cup chopped pecans
Glaze
½ cup whisky
½ cup (1 stick) butter or margarine
¾ cup sugar

For cake: Preheat oven to 325°F. Grease and flour a 10-inch tube pan.

Mix all ingredients in large bowl. Pour batter into pan. Bake 55 minutes. Place pan on rack; loosen sides with knife. Do not remove from pan.

For glaze: In 3-cup saucepan, combine all ingredients. Cook over medium heat, stirring frequently until blended. Simmer until ready to use; pour over top and down sides of warm cake. When cake is cool, remove from pan and slice in wedges.

One only eats well at home.

Anonymous, French saying

Cheesecakes

Betty R. Hunter
Louisville, Kentucky
Kentucky Cardinals Sams

When it's Betty's turn to supply dessert for a chapter potluck but it's just too hot to turn on the RV oven, she whips up this creamy cheesecake. RV cooks will love it because it's so easy to prepare.

Serves 12

Cheesecake Supreme

3 cups graham cracker crumbs
½ cup (1 stick) butter or margarine, melted
1 cup boiling water
1 3-ounce package lemon gelatin
1 cup sugar
1 8-ounce package cream cheese
1 teaspoon vanilla
1 12-ounce can evaporated milk, chilled

Mix 2 cups graham cracker crumbs with melted butter. Spread evenly on bottom of 10 × 12-inch baking pan. In medium bowl, dissolve gelatin in water; allow to cool. Add sugar, cream cheese, and vanilla and beat until well blended.

In small bowl, beat evaporated milk until thick. Add to cream cheese mixture; blend well. Spread over graham cracker crust. Sprinkle remaining crumbs on top of mixture. Chill for 2 hours before serving.

Karen Waterman
Nashua, Iowa
Wapsi Valley Sams

If Karen plans to prepare this for an RV outing, she takes along her springform pan. The compliments you get will make it well worth the effort of making this rich and creamy special-occasion dessert.

Serves 12

German Cheesecake

Crust

1¼ cups flour

1 teaspoon baking powder

⅓ cup sugar

2 tablespoons (¼ stick) butter or margarine, softened

1 egg yolk, beaten

5 tablespoons milk

Filling

2 egg yolks

¾ cup plus 1 tablespoon sugar

Grated rind of 1 large lemon

Juice of 1 large lemon

2 8-ounce packages cream cheese

2 tablespoons vanilla pudding mix (not instant)

⅓ cup milk

½ cup cornstarch

3 egg whites

For crust: Preheat oven to 375°F. In medium bowl, mix flour, baking powder, and sugar; cut in butter as if mixing pie crust. Add remaining ingredients and mix thoroughly. Press mixture on bottom and 1 inch up sides of 10½-inch springform pan; dough will be sticky.

For filling: Put egg yolks, sugar, grated lemon rind, lemon juice, and 1 package cream cheese in blender; blend on medium speed until smooth. Add remaining cream cheese, pudding, milk, and cornstarch; blend.

Beat egg whites until they hold stiff peaks. Add blender mixture slowly, folding into egg whites. Do not beat.

Pour filling over crust mixture. Bake 1 hour.

Kathleen Daymude
Anchorage, Alaska
Sourdough Sams

Since Kathleen's cheesecake freezes well, she finds it's a great way to have a home-cooked dessert on hand for unexpected guests. It's terrific for both summer outings and winter potlucks.

Serves 20

Alaska Cheesecake

Crust
2½ cups graham cracker crumbs
¼ cup sugar
½ cup (1 stick) butter or margarine, softened
Filling
5 8-ounce packages cream cheese, softened
1¾ cups sugar
3 tablespoons flour
Peel of 1 lemon, grated, or 1 teaspoon lemon juice
¼ teaspoon vanilla
5 eggs
2 egg yolks
¼ cup heavy cream
½ cup sour cream (optional)

For crust: In medium bowl, mix graham cracker crumbs with sugar and butter. Press mixture on bottom and sides of a 12-inch springform pan, building up sides about halfway to top of pan. Refrigerate until needed.

For filling: Preheat oven to 500°F. In large bowl, combine cream cheese, sugar, flour, lemon peel (or juice), and vanilla. Beat at high speed until blended. Beat in eggs and egg yolks one at a time. Add heavy cream and beat until blended. Pour into crust. Bake 10 minutes, then reduce oven to 250°F and continue to bake 45 minutes. Filling will be soft in the middle when removed from oven, but will set as it cools. Let cool in pan on wire rack; refrigerate at least 3 hours. If desired, top with sour cream.

To serve, loosen crust from sides of pan. Remove sides of pan; cut cheesecake into wedges to serve.

Hint: For variety, top with fruit.

Dolores Bristol
Milford, Connecticut
Wepawaug Sams

This sugarless recipe not only tastes good, it's super-easy because there's no baking. The recipe can be varied by taking advantage of the many available pie fillings.

Serves 12

Ladyfinger Cheesecake

1 pint whipping cream
2 8-ounce packages cream cheese, softened
3 0.3-ounce packages ladyfingers, without filling
1 21-ounce can pie filling, your choice

In small bowl, whip cream until stiff peaks form. In medium bowl, beat cream cheese until smooth. Add whipped cream to cream cheese and continue to beat until blended.

Line springform pan with ladyfingers, sides first, then bottom. (Place flat sides of ladyfingers toward inside.) Pour half of creamed mixture into pan. Add another layer of ladyfingers; top with remaining mixture. Spread pie filling on top and refrigerate 2 hours or until ready to serve.

'Tis the dessert that graces all the feast,
For an ill end disparages the rest:
Make your transparent sweet-meats
   timely rise,
With Indian sugar and Arabian spice;
And let your various creams enriched be
With swelling fruit just ravished from
   the tree....

Anonymous, *Apician Morsels*

Chilled Desserts

Virginia Cummins
Punta Gorda, Florida
Gulf Coast Sams

Virginia's dessert is delicious and easily adapted to various fruits in season. It's also easy to prepare.

Serves 12

Chocolate Dream

1 cup flour
½ cup (1 stick) butter or margarine, softened
1 cup chopped nuts
1 cup confectioners sugar
1 8-ounce package cream cheese, softened
1 12-ounce container whipped topping
1 3½-ounce package instant vanilla or butter brickle pudding mix
1 3½-ounce package instant chocolate pudding mix
2 cups milk
Crushed toffee bar, chocolate bar, or chopped nuts for garnish

Preheat oven to 350°F.

Combine flour and butter; add nuts. Press into 9 × 13-inch baking pan. Bake 20 minutes; allow to cool.

Mix confectioners sugar with cream cheese; add 1 cup of whipped topping. Spread over crust.

Beat instant puddings with milk; spread over second layer. Cover with remaining whipped topping. Sprinkle with garnish. Refrigerate before serving.

Hint: In place of pudding layer, use sliced strawberries, bananas, and peaches mixed with strawberry glaze.

Lucy Hyden
Sardis,
  British Columbia,
  Canada
Chilliwack Valley Sams

The smooth texture and rich flavor of Lucy's chilled float make it suitable for a mid-afternoon pick-me-up or after-dinner dessert. Standard ingredients make it a natural for RVers.

Serves 8

Almond Float

| 2 tablespoons unflavored gelatin |
| 1/4 cup cold water |
| 2/3 cup sugar |
| 3 cups milk, scalded |
| 1 teaspoon almond extract |
| 1 15 1/4-ounce can tropical fruit cocktail, drained |
| 1 11-ounce can mandarin oranges, drained |

In medium bowl, combine gelatin and cold water; stir well. Add sugar to scalded milk and bring to boil. Pour into gelatin mixture and add almond extract. Pour mixture into 8 × 8-inch pan and chill. Add fruit to top of mixture 1 hour before serving.

Judy Racine
Stratford, Connecticut
Wepawaug Sams

We like to think of the winter holidays as a time for the distinctive taste of cranberries, but Judy's cranberry cream would make a great summer treat.

Serves 8

Cranberry Cream

| 2 1/4-ounce packages unflavored gelatin |
| 3 3/4 cups cranberry-raspberry juice |
| 1 cup sour cream |
| 1 cup heavy cream, whipped |

Soften each package of gelatin separately in 1/2 cup juice. In small pan, heat 1 1/2 cups juice; dissolve one of the gelatin mixtures in heated juice, stirring until cool. Pour into bowl; refrigerate until jelled.

Heat remaining juice (1 1/4 cups); add to remaining portion of softened gelatin; stir until dissolved. Cool. Add sour cream and beat until well mixed. Pour over jelled mixture and return to refrigerator until top layer has jelled. Top with whipped cream; garnish as desired.

Hint: *For a pretty party dish, use a clear glass bowl to display the layers. For garnishes, try chocolate curls, sprinkles, orange slices, or mint leaves.*

Doris V. McAdams
Santa Rosa, California
Clover Country Sams

After tasting a fruit-basket cake from a bakery that specialized in fancy desserts, Doris decided to do some experimenting so she could serve her own version of this treat. Now it's in popular demand at chapter camp-outs, and disappears too fast to even consider having any for leftovers.

Serves 20

Fruit Sundae Cake

1 18.25-ounce package pineapple cake mix
1 cup sugar
1 20-ounce can crushed pineapple, juice reserved
4 large bananas, sliced
1 20-ounce jar orange marmalade
1 5¼-ounce package instant vanilla pudding mix
4 cups milk
2 baskets strawberries, stemmed, halved, or sliced
1 8-ounce package cream cheese, softened
1 pint whipping cream
2 cups chopped walnuts
1 20-ounce jar maraschino cherries, drained and halved

Grease and flour 9 × 13 × 2-inch pan. Bake cake according to directions on package. While cake is baking, mix sugar into pineapple and set aside.

Remove cake from oven and cool on rack, leaving cake in pan. When cool enough to handle, press cake down as flat as possible; prick top with fork. Pour ½ of reserved pineapple juice over cake. With slotted spoon, add crushed pineapple, spreading evenly over cake. Arrange thick layer of sliced bananas over pineapple, then spread orange marmalade over bananas.

Mix pudding with electric beater, using 4 cups of milk instead of 3 as directed on package. Before it thickens, pour pudding evenly over cake. Let stand about 10 minutes for pudding to thicken. Add layer of strawberries, overlapping to cover.

With electric mixer, beat cream cheese until smooth. In separate bowl, beat whipping cream until stiff. Fold cream cheese into whipping cream until well blended. Cover top of cake with this mixture. Sprinkle with nuts and press cherry halves into top, round side up. Cover with aluminum foil and refrigerate overnight.

Clara Lee Snowden
Charleston, South Carolina
Trident Sams

Your Good Sam friends will be
convinced you're a professional
caterer when you show up at a
potluck with this delicious dessert.
Offered in a glass bowl, it's almost
too pretty to eat.

Serves 12

Jack's Macaroon Delight

1 19-ounce package macaroons
1½ cups milk
1 15½-ounce can crushed pineapple, drained
1 12-ounce container whipped topping
¾ cup chopped nuts

Dip each macaroon in milk quickly and layer bottom and sides of deep serving dish. Spread ½ of pineapple over macaroons. Spoon thick layer of whipped topping over pineapple. Repeat macaroon-pineapple layer. Fill dish to top with alternating layers of macaroons and whipped topping. Garnish with nuts. Cover and refrigerate overnight.

Hint: When serving, push spoon straight down to bottom of dish.

Betty Heryet
Williams Lake,
　British Columbia,
　Canada
Cariboo Sams

Are you looking for a different
dessert for a potluck dinner? Betty's
Lemon Bisque feeds 20 hungry Good
Samers and can be prepared at
home, giving the chef plenty of time
to socialize.

Serves 20

Lemon Bisque

1 3-ounce package lemon gelatin
1¾ cups boiling water
2 cups graham cracker crumbs
¼ cup (½ stick) butter or margarine
1 12-ounce can evaporated milk, chilled
2 tablespoons lemon juice
1 cup sugar

Dissolve lemon gelatin in boiling water and let stand until partially jelled. Blend graham cracker crumbs with melted butter. Butter 9 × 13-inch pan; spread crumbs evenly over bottom of pan.

Beat evaporated milk with lemon juice and sugar until thick; add to lemon gelatin, beating until well blended. Pour over crumb mixture; chill.

Barbara L. Savage
Bath, Maine
Member at Large

This recipe can be varied just by changing the flavor of pudding each time you prepare it. Barbara prefers chocolate, but any flavor of instant pudding will give it a new color and taste.

Serves 10 to 12

Pudding Promise

Crust

½ cup (1 stick) butter or margarine

1 cup flour

½ cup chopped pecans

Filling

1 cup confectioners sugar

1 8-ounce package cream cheese, softened

1 12-ounce container whipped topping,
1½ cups reserved

Topping

1 5¼-ounce package chocolate instant pudding mix or
your choice

For crust: Preheat oven to 350°F. Cream together butter and flour; add pecans. Pat into bottom of 8 × 11-inch baking pan. Bake 10 minutes. Cool.

For filling: Cream together sugar and cream cheese; fold in whipped topping. Spread mixture on crust.

For topping: Mix pudding, following directions on package. Spread over cream cheese mixture. Add reserved topping.

If desired, garnish with shaved chocolate, nuts, or fruit, depending on flavor selected for topping. Refrigerate until ready to serve.

The proof of the pudding is in the eating.

Henry Glapthorne, *The Hollander,* 1635

Loretta Clark
Sumter, South Carolina
Sams of Sumter

Loretta's cake really isn't made or served in a punch bowl, but when the layers of cake, strawberries, pudding, and whipped topping are all stacked and ready to serve, it's pretty enough for your holiday table.

Serves 20

Punch Bowl Cake

| 1 1.25-pound box yellow cake mix |
| 1 quart strawberries, stemmed and sliced (reserve 6 for garnish) |
| 2 3½-ounce packages instant vanilla pudding mix |
| 1 12-ounce container whipped topping |

Bake cake in two layers as directed on package. While cake is baking, make instant pudding as directed on package.

After cake has cooled, slice each of the layers into two. Starting with one of the layers, place, in order, cake, strawberries, pudding, and whipped topping. Repeat four times, ending with whipped topping. Garnish with remaining strawberries. Refrigerate for 1 to 2 hours and serve.

Jean S. Huett
Riviera, Arizona
Colorado River Roamers

Although Jean's wonderful, rich-tasting dessert can be prepared in 15 minutes and requires no cooking, it will make an elegant finale to a company dinner.

Serves 15 to 18

No-Bake Chocolate-Graham Torte

| 1 16-ounce package whole graham crackers |
| 2 3½-ounce packages instant vanilla pudding mix |
| 3 cups milk |
| 1 8- or 10-ounce container whipped topping |
| 1 16-ounce can milk chocolate frosting |
| 3 teaspoons milk |

Line the bottom of a 9 × 13-inch baking pan with one layer of graham crackers. Mix pudding with milk, then stir in whipped topping. Spread ½ of mixture over graham crackers. Repeat layers, starting and ending with graham crackers.

Mix chocolate frosting with 3 teaspoons milk. Spread mixture over last layer of graham crackers. Refrigerate overnight. Cut into individual pieces to serve.

Mae Jones
Chesapeake, Virginia
Virginia Good Sam Rebels

Mae's prize-winning recipe can be used as a dessert or a side dish, especially for a holiday dinner. A food processor would come in handy for grating the sweet potatoes, but grandma managed without one and so can RVers.

Serves 10 to 12

Grated Sweet Potato Pudding

½ cup (1 stick) butter or margarine

4 cups grated sweet potatoes

1½ cups brown sugar

2 cups milk or cream diluted with water

½ cup chopped nuts

½ cup flour

½ teaspoon baking soda

1 teaspoon nutmeg

1 teaspoon vanilla

2 eggs, beaten

Preheat oven to 350°F. Melt butter in 9 × 13-inch baking pan. In large bowl, mix all ingredients together, adding eggs last. Pour mixture into baking dish; bake 40 to 50 minutes. Midway through baking time, when crust forms around edges and top of mixture, remove from oven, stir, and return to oven for remaining baking time (crust will form again). Serve warm or chilled.

Hint: For variety, before baking add ¾ cup coconut or ¾ cup raisins.

All food is the gift of the gods and has something of the miraculous, the egg no less than the truffle.

Sybille Bedford

Lynne H. Jerard
Albany, New York
Tri City Sams

Lynne took her mother's recipe and, after making a few changes, found it "sinfully" good, and so will Good Samers. It's a chocolate-lover's delight and should be served in small pieces because it's also sinfully rich.

Serves 25

Lynne's Sin

Brownie Base

3 eggs

¾ cup (1½ sticks) plus 3 tablespoons butter
or margarine, softened

1½ cups sugar

9 tablespoons cocoa

¾ cup all purpose flour

¾ cup chopped walnuts

Topping

6 tablespoons (¾ stick) butter or margarine, softened

3½ cups confectioners sugar

3 tablespoons milk

1 teaspoon vanilla

Glaze

9 tablespoons cocoa

6 tablespoons (¾ stick) butter or margarine

For brownie base: Preheat oven to 350°F. In medium bowl, beat eggs until frothy. In small bowl, cream butter and sugar; add to eggs. Mix cocoa, flour, and nuts together. Add to first mixture and stir until well blended. Pour into 9 × 9-inch baking pan that has been coated with nonstick baking spray. Bake 15 to 30 minutes, until a toothpick inserted in the center comes out clean; *do not overbake.* Cool thoroughly before adding topping.
For topping: In small bowl, blend all ingredients well. Spread over cooled brownie base. Let stand at least 10 minutes before adding glaze.
For glaze: Stir cocoa into softened butter. Pour over topping, tilting pan so glaze covers entire base. Refrigerate 15 minutes.

Hint: In preparing brownie base, mix nuts with flour before adding to other mixture; this will prevent nuts from sinking to bottom during baking. Don't overbake; this base gets hard quickly.

Cookies

Gladys Howe
Junction City, Kansas
J.C. Truckin Sams

Gladys's easy no-bake cookies are so popular that she often makes a double batch. The rich honey-and-peanut butter taste calls for a tall glass of cold milk or cup of steaming coffee or tea.

Serves 6

Helen Mogg
Corunna, Michigan
Rolling Eagles

Helen's unusual cookies are crisp and crunchy. It's a great way to finish off a bag of leftover potato chips.

Makes 1½ dozen

Almond Delight

1 5-ounce package almond bark
30 snack crackers (Gladys prefers Ritz)
¾ cup smooth peanut butter

Melt almond bark in double boiler. Spread peanut butter between two crackers. Repeat with remaining crackers. Dip crackers in melted almond bark. Arrange on waxed paper until cooled.

Helen's Potato Chip Cookies

¾ cup (1½ sticks) butter or margarine
2 cups firmly packed brown sugar
2 eggs
3 cups flour
½ teaspoon baking soda
⅓ cup milk
1 cup potato chips
2 teaspoons vanilla
1 cup chopped nuts (optional)

Preheat oven to 350°F.
Cream all ingredients together and drop by teaspoonfuls onto greased baking sheet. Bake 10 to 15 minutes.

Grace Almond
Englewood, Colorado
Member at Large

Grace's unique recipe has won more than one cooking contest and is sure to please Good Samers gathered for coffee and treats. These lemony brownies, topped with a cream cheese frosting, are deliciously different.

Serves 20

Lemon Brownies

Brownies

½ cup (1 stick) butter or margarine

2 cups brown sugar, firmly packed

3 eggs

2 teaspoons lemon flavoring

1½ cups presifted flour

1 cup quick oats

1 teaspoon baking powder (double acting)

½ teaspoon salt

¾ cup buttermilk

1 7-ounce package lemon chips

⅔ cup pecans, coarsely chopped

Frosting

1 8-ounce package cream cheese

¼ cup (½ stick) butter or margarine

1 1-pound box confectioners sugar

1 tablespoon flour

Pinch salt

1 teaspoon vanilla

For brownies: Preheat oven to 350°F. Grease and flour a 10 × 15-inch jelly roll pan. In a 2-quart mixing bowl, cream butter and brown sugar until light and fluffy. Continue to beat, adding eggs and lemon flavoring.

Stir in dry ingredients alternately with buttermilk, beginning and ending with dry ingredients. Blend in lemon chips and pecans.

Spoon into prepared pan and spread evenly. Bake 25 minutes or until toothpick inserted in center comes out clean. Cool.

For frosting: Mix ingredients in order listed and beat until fluffy. Spread evenly over cooled brownies. Cut into bars.

Carole Beek
Winnipeg, Manitoba, Canada
Manitoba Sunny Sams

Lemon Squares

These bars taste like lemon meringue pie, but have a texture and crust all their own. See Carole's hints about how to plan ahead and save time for socializing when preparing this at your next camp-out.

Makes 9 large or 25 small squares

Crust

½ cup (1 stick) butter or margarine, softened

¼ cup confectioners sugar

1 cup all purpose flour

Filling

2 eggs

1 cup sugar

½ teaspoon baking powder

¼ teaspoon salt

2 tablespoons lemon juice

For crust: Preheat oven to 350°F. In a medium bowl, cream butter. Work in confectioners sugar. Gradually add flour, being sure to combine all ingredients thoroughly. Mixture will be very stiff; you may have to work in last of the flour with your hands.

Press mixture into bottom of ungreased 8×8-inch or 9×9-inch pan. Pat down evenly. Bake 20 minutes.

For filling: In medium bowl, beat eggs until whites and yolks are well blended. Add sugar, baking powder, salt, and lemon juice. Beat for 3 minutes or until light and fluffy. Pour over hot crust. Bake for 25 minutes or until imprint remains when touched lightly in center. Cool and cut into squares.

Hint: When preparing for an outing, carry premeasured and pre-mixed flour and confectioners sugar in one container and sugar, baking powder, and salt in another; the rest will be easy.

Next to eating good dinners, a healthy man with a benevolent turn of mind, must like, I think, to read about them.

William Thackeray

Phyllis Elrod
Wichita, Kansas
Aero Sams

This attractive cookie is easy to prepare and store, and comes in handy when guests drop in for coffee. The cookies can be made in two sizes, by using either conventional size or small muffin tins. The recipe captured the attention of judges at the Kansas State Samboree Cook-off.

Makes 2 dozen

Peanut Butter Temptations

½ cup (1 stick) butter or margarine, softened
½ cup peanut butter (either smooth or crunchy)
½ cup sugar
½ cup firmly packed brown sugar
1 egg
1¼ cups flour
¾ teaspoon baking soda
½ teaspoon salt
1 8-ounce package Reese's Peanut Butter Pieces

Preheat oven to 375°F. In large bowl, cream butter, peanut butter, and sugars. Beat in egg.

Mix dry ingredients together and add to creamed mixture. Roll into 1-inch balls (or ½-inch balls for small muffin pan) and place in greased muffin pans. Bake 8 to 10 minutes.

Remove from oven and immediately put one peanut butter piece in center of each cookie, pressing it down. Let stand 10 minutes before removing from pan.

Hint: When using small muffin pans, cut peanut butter pieces in half before pressing into cookies.

Marcella C. Hull
Chester, Montana
Milk River Good Sams

What could be easier than stirring up a batch of Marcella's easy unbaked cookies? Great to make up ahead of a trip, or even on the road.

Makes 40 cookies

Unbaked Chocolate Goodies

4 cups cornflakes
1 cup flaked coconut
1 cup chopped nuts or raisins
1 6-ounce package semisweet chocolate chips
1 1-ounce square unsweetened chocolate
1 14-ounce can sweetened condensed milk

Combine cornflakes, coconut, and chopped nuts or raisins in a large mixing bowl and toss. Set aside.

Melt chocolate chips and unsweetened chocolate in a double boiler over hot water (it will take about 10 minutes to melt). When melted, add milk; mix well. Pour chocolate mixture over cornflake mixture and stir until all dry ingredients are incorporated. Drop by teaspoonfuls onto waxed paper and allow to set until firm. Turn cookies over after tops have firmed to allow bottoms to harden. Store in airtight container.

Dorothy Urban
Morganville, Kansas
Piotigue Sams

Dorothy worked this recipe out in her mind one night when she couldn't sleep. After she tried it, her family decided she should stay awake more often to dream up other recipes. So did the judges at the Kansas State Samboree Cook-off.

Makes about 2 dozen

Praline Sugar Cookies

½ cup firmly packed brown sugar
½ cup confectioners sugar
½ cup oil
½ cup (1 stick) butter or margarine, softened
1 egg
1 teaspoon vanilla
2 cups plus 1 tablespoon flour, unsifted
½ teaspoon salt
½ teaspoon baking soda
½ teaspoon cream of tartar
½ cup finely chopped pecans

Preheat oven to 350°F. Cream first 6 ingredients together until fluffy. Add dry ingredients and nuts to creamed mixture.

Drop by teaspoonfuls onto ungreased cookie sheet; flatten with glass that has been dipped in sugar. Bake for 8 minutes.

Hint: For variation, leave out nuts or add coconut.

Opal A. Steinbeck
Grand Island, Nebraska
Platte Valley Sams

Opal picked up this recipe from a friend in Montana and found it a quick and easy snack to keep on hand to serve after an evening around the campfire or at a dance.

Yield depends on serving size

Rhubarb Bars

| 3 cups diced rhubarb |
| 1½ cups sugar |
| 1 teaspoon vanilla |
| 2 tablespoons cornstarch, dissolved in ¼ cup cold water |
| 1½ cups oatmeal |
| 1½ cups sifted flour |
| 1 cup firmly packed brown sugar |
| ½ teaspoon baking soda |
| 1 cup (2 sticks) butter or margarine |
| ½ cup chopped walnuts |

Preheat oven to 350°F. In large pan, mix rhubarb, sugar, and vanilla. Add cornstarch. Cook over low heat until rhubarb is tender, stirring constantly until thickened. Set aside to cool.

In medium bowl, mix dry ingredients; cut in butter. Add nuts and combine well.

Pat ¾ of crumb mixture in 9 × 13-inch pan. Add cooled rhubarb. Sprinkle remaining crumbs on top. Bake 40 minutes. Serve warm or chilled.

Shirley Townsend
Fremont, New Hampshire
Swinging Puckerbrushes

Shirley's delicious cookies need no baking—everything is prepared on top of the stove. They keep well in covered containers, too.

Makes 3 dozen

Coconut-Date Rolls

| 8 ounces pitted dates |
| 1 cup sugar |
| ½ cup (1 stick) margarine or butter |
| 1 egg, beaten |
| 1 teaspoon vanilla |
| 2½ cups rice cereal (Rice Krispies work best) |
| Shredded coconut for coating |

Mix dates, sugar, margarine or butter, and egg in large saucepan. Cook over medium heat until sugar is dissolved and dates are softened. Add vanilla and rice cereal and mix well.

Drop by teaspoonfuls onto waxed paper spread with coconut. Roll each cookie in coconut until well covered on all sides.

Rosalee J. Rittle
Augusta, Kansas
Conestoga Campers

Rosalee's grandmother baked these cookies when she lived on a farm and had all of the fresh cream and eggs she needed. The family even had their wheat ground into flour. Grandma would add whatever she had on hand to her basic recipe, and sometimes she frosted the cookies. Rosalee recalls that the cookies never lasted very long after they came out of the oven.

Makes 5 to 6 dozen

Grandma's Farm Cookies

1 cup cream
1 cup sugar
2 eggs
1 teaspoon vanilla
1 teaspoon baking soda
1 teaspoon baking powder
3½ cups flour
Nuts, candied fruit, bananas, coconut, chocolate chips, peanut butter chips, butterscotch chips, or any desired addition

Preheat oven to 400°F. Mix cream and sugar; add and beat in eggs and vanilla. Stir in dry ingredients. Add any of the optional ingredients.

Drop on ungreased cookie sheet by rounded teaspoonfuls. Bake 10 minutes.

Cookies may be frosted with your own recipe or prepared frosting, if desired.

Dorothy M. Fleagle
Enterprise, Kansas
Twin Dams Sams

Dorothy finds this peanut butter-flavored cookie recipe perfect for RVers because there's nothing to mix. It's also popular with those lucky enough to be around when these treats come out of the oven.

Makes 48 cookies

Cookies in a Cup

---

1 20-ounce package refrigerated
peanut butter cookie dough

---

1 8-ounce package miniature
peanut butter cup candies

Preheat oven to 350°F. Slice roll of prepared cookie dough into thirds, cut each third into four pieces, and cut each of these pieces into fourths for a total of 48. Put pieces into small muffin tins and bake 8 to 12 minutes; centers will drop while baking.

Remove from oven and place a peanut butter candy into center of each cookie. Let cool before removing from pan.

Hint: *Cookies will be easier to remove if baking pan is coated with nonstick baking spray or if paper baking cups are used.*

Pies

Judy Kerr
Arlington, Texas
Good Sambinos

Chess pie, legend has it, got its name from a plantation cook who, when asked what she was making, answered, "Jus' pie." Judy's recipe is from the Tennessee mountains and has been served at her family's holiday dinners for over 50 years.

Serves 8 to 10

Aunt Rachel's Chess Pie

½ cup (1 stick) butter
3 eggs
2 cups sugar
2 tablespoons yellow cornmeal
5 tablespoons buttermilk
Pinch of salt
1 teaspoon vanilla
1 9-inch unbaked pie shell

Preheat oven to 350°F. Melt butter and set aside to cool.

Beat eggs well. Add sugar and beat again, using electric or hand mixer. Add cornmeal, buttermilk, and salt; stir well. Add butter and vanilla and beat again.

Pour into unbaked pie shell and bake about 30 to 40 minutes, until toothpick inserted in center comes out clean. Test every 5 minutes after 30 minutes of baking. Do not try to speed up cooking time as filling will not set. Remove from oven and cool.

Promises and pie-crusts are made
to be broken.

Jonathan Swift, *Polite Conversations*, 1738

Jo Golay
Dauphin, Manitoba, Canada
Parkland Sams

Jo's unusual dessert pizza features fresh fruits in abundance, glazed with a lemon-orange mixture over a creamy base. It would make a spectacular holiday centerpiece.

Serves 6 to 8

Fruited Pizza

Crust

½ cup confectioners sugar

¾ cup cold butter

1½ cups flour

Cheese Layer

1 8-ounce package cream cheese

1 teaspoon vanilla

1 cup sugar

Fruit Layer

Oranges, pineapple, bananas, strawberries, or any fresh fruit in season, sliced

Glaze

2 tablespoons cornstarch

½ cup sugar

1 teaspoon lemon juice

1 cup orange juice

1 teaspoon vanilla

For crust: Preheat oven to 300°F. Mix sugar, butter, and flour together. Blend with pastry blender. Pat into a buttered pizza pan and bake until edges turn light brown, about 8 to 10 minutes.

For cheese layer: Mix cream cheese, vanilla, and sugar together and spread over cooled crust.

For fruit layer: Arrange sliced fruits (enough to cover top of pizza) in swirl pattern over top of cheese layer.

For glaze: Mix the cornstarch and sugar together. Add lemon juice, orange juice, and vanilla. Heat in small saucepan, stirring constantly, until thickened. Cool.

For finished pizza: Spread glaze over fruit. (Glaze also will prevent fruit from darkening.) Refrigerate 4 to 6 hours or overnight. Slice and serve.

Honorable Mention

Joyce H. Wise
Chagrin Falls, Ohio
Willoughby Highway Sams

Joyce's easy-to-make-and-bake recipe scores with Good Samers who find it suitable for an RV galley. It has the flavor of pecan pie, but is easier to make and not as rich.

Serves 8

Japanese Fruit Pie

½ cup (1 stick) butter or margarine, melted
1 cup sugar
2 eggs, beaten
½ cup flaked coconut
½ cup chopped pecans or walnuts
½ cup raisins
1 teaspoon white vinegar
1 9-inch unbaked pie shell

Preheat oven to 350°F. Pour butter into medium bowl. Add ingredients to butter, one at a time; mix well. Pour into pie shell and bake for 30 to 40 minutes.

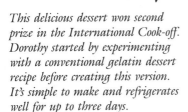

Second Prize

Dorothy M. Jennings
San Jose, California
Camino Cavaliers

This delicious dessert won second prize in the International Cook-off. Dorothy started by experimenting with a conventional gelatin dessert recipe before creating this version. It's simple to make and refrigerates well for up to three days.

Serves 8

Pineapple Sour Cream Pie

1 5¼-ounce package instant vanilla pudding mix
1 8-ounce can crushed pineapple, including juice
1 tablespoon sugar
1 pint sour cream
1 9-inch prepared graham cracker crust
Whipped cream or topping for garnish

In a large bowl, combine pudding mix, pineapple, sugar, and sour cream. Mix well, but do not use electric mixer. Pour into crust and refrigerate for 2 hours. Top with whipped cream or whipped topping, if desired.

Hint: *To cut down on calories, Dorothy suggests using a sugar substitute. She also uses a prepared, unrefrigerated pie crust because it comes wrapped for storage.*

Delno H. Moore
Kalispell, Montana
Flathead Valley Sams

Del claims this is the best raspberry pie in the country, and Good Samers might agree. The RV chef will certainly find that it is one of the easiest desserts to prepare in a small galley.

Serves 6

Del's Raspberry Pie

3 cups raspberries
¾ cup sugar
2 tablespoons tapioca
Dash of cinnamon
2 8-inch unbaked pie shells

Preheat oven to 400°F. Mix all ingredients together; pour into pie shell; top with second crust. Bake 1 hour.

Hint: *For best results, use ripe, fresh raspberries.*

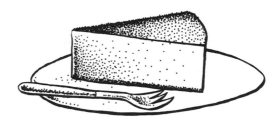

There is something in the red of a raspberry pie that looks as good to a man as the red in a sheep looks to a wolf.

E. W. Howe, *Sinner Sermons,* 1926

Marjorie Brand
San Marcos, California
Weekend Rollers

Marjorie was searching through her motorhome galley one day to see what she could "throw together" for an impromptu potluck with some RVing friends. The result was this delicious pie. Her friends weren't the only ones who liked her discovery; it was one of the three winning recipes at the Northern California State Samboree Cook-off.

Serves 6 to 8

Tropical Cream Pie

| 1 8-ounce container whipped topping (Marjorie prefers La Creme) |
| 1 3-ounce package orange-flavored gelatin |
| 1 11-ounce can mandarin oranges, drained |
| 1 15½-ounce can pineapple tidbits, drained |
| 1 large banana, sliced |
| 1 9-inch prepared graham cracker crust |
| Mint leaves or chocolate curls for garnish |

Let whipped topping thaw for ½ hour in its own container. Turn into medium mixing bowl and whip with a fork until the topping is fluffy and free of lumps.

Slowly add dry gelatin to topping, beating continuously until the gelatin is mostly dissolved.

Add oranges, pineapple, and banana; stir to distribute evenly. Pour into crust and chill 1 hour in freezer or until firmly set. Garnish with mint or chocolate.

Candies

Anna P. Pence
Richmond, Virginia
First Virginians

The smooth peanut butter fudge is topped with a creamy frosting in Anna's delightful candy.

Makes approximately 30 pieces

Cloud-topped Peanut Butter Fudge

Fudge

1 cup evaporated milk

2 cups sugar

1 teaspoon salt

¼ cup (½ stick) butter

2 cups peanut butter morsels

Topping

½ cup firmly packed brown sugar

6 tablespoons (¾ stick) butter

½ cup corn syrup

2 cups sifted confectioners sugar

1 cup chopped walnuts

For fudge: In heavy saucepan, combine evaporated milk, sugar, salt, and butter. Bring to boil over moderate heat and boil 8 minutes, stirring constantly. Remove from heat and add peanut butter morsels. Stir until morsels melt and mixture is smooth. Spread into a foil-lined 9-inch-square pan and chill 30 minutes. **For topping:** In heavy saucepan, combine brown sugar, butter, and corn syrup. Stir over low heat until smooth. Bring to boil and remove from heat. Add sugar and walnuts. Stir until well blended. Spread over chilled fudge. Chill again until firm.

Anna P. Pence
Richmond, Virginia
First Virginians

Anna loves fudge and her easy chocolate version will satisfy the sweet tooth of any chocoholic.

Makes 50 or more pieces

Easy Chocolate Fudge

½ cup (1 stick) butter or margarine
1 6-ounce package semisweet chocolate chips
1 teaspoon vanilla
2 cups sugar
1 5⅓-ounce can evaporated milk
10 marshmallows
1 cup chopped nuts

Combine butter, chocolate, and vanilla in medium bowl. Mix well and set aside.

Mix together sugar, milk, and marshmallows in medium saucepan. Cook over medium heat until mixture comes to boil. Reduce heat and continue cooking, stirring constantly for 6 minutes.

Pour hot syrup over butter-chocolate mixture. Beat by hand or with electric mixer until fudge is thick and loses its shiny gloss. Stir in nuts.

Pour into greased 8-inch-square pan. Refrigerate several hours until firm. Cut into small squares.

Priscilla D. Rondeau
Mendon, Massachusetts
Friendship Sams International

As far as Priscilla can determine, this recipe has always been in her family. Several magazines have published it because it's so unusual and simple to make. It's hard to believe potato is an ingredient!

Makes 64 1-inch pieces

Potato Candy

1 medium potato, cooked
1 4-ounce package coconut
1 1-pound box confectioners sugar
¼ cup peanut butter
1 1-ounce square unsweetened chocolate, melted

While cooked potato is still warm, mash and add coconut, sugar, and peanut butter. Mix until well blended.

Spread into an 8-inch buttered baking pan, pressing smooth with a fork. Spread melted chocolate evenly over top. Refrigerate to set. Cut into 1-inch pieces.

Ruby Walker
Lubbock, Texas
Sandhill Sams

*Ruby has made this old family
recipe for years at parties and
chapter picnics. A taffy pull is fun
for adults and it's particularly good
for keeping children busy.*

Makes approximately 1 dozen pieces

Old-fashioned Taffy

3 cups sugar
1 cup white corn syrup
1 cup water
¼ cup (½ stick) butter
⅓ cup vinegar
1 tablespoon vanilla

Mix sugar, syrup, and water in a 4-quart saucepan and place over medium heat. **Do not stir.** Cook until mixture reaches soft-ball stage. Add butter, vinegar, and vanilla. Cook again until mixture reaches hard-ball stage. Again, **do not stir.**

Pour out onto 3 greased platters and begin to pull. Keep hands lubricated with butter and pull the taffy with a partner. Pull until the candy turns light and cools. The more the candy is pulled, the better it will be. Place on chopping block and cut into pieces with a knife.

Hint: This is a great icebreaker at a camp-out. The taffy can be cooked inside the RV and then taken outside for pulling.

Paula Boone Gough
Lubbock, Texas
Cotton Pickin Sams

*An easy, crunchy candy that will
disappear in minutes, Paula's
confection also is good to make
ahead and store (if you can).*

Makes about 30 squares

Heavenly Hash

1 pound whole pecans
Salt to taste (optional)
1 16-ounce package large marshmallows, each piece cut into 5 smaller pieces
2 12-ounce packages semisweet chocolate chips
½ cup (1 stick) butter or margarine

Toast pecans in oven for 1 hour at 250°F. Salt generously while roasting and stir often.

Melt chocolate chips and margarine in top of double boiler. Mix together ½ of the marshmallows and toasted pecans. Add

½ of the chocolate mixture. Mix well. Add the remaining marshmallows, pecans, and chocolate and stir well. Spread into a greased 9 × 13-inch pan and allow to set in refrigerator. When firm, cut into squares.

Hint: Use a knife dipped in warm water or flour to cut the marshmallows into pieces.

Barbara J. Fogg
Oak Hill, Florida
Member at Large

Barbara's very simple candy only takes a few minutes to prepare, and it's so good.

Serves 8

Quick Peanut-Chocolate Fudge

1 8-ounce package chocolate chips
1 cup (2 sticks) butter or margarine
12 ounces chunky peanut butter
1 1-pound box confectioners sugar
1 teaspoon vanilla

In 3-quart saucepan, melt chocolate chips and butter or margarine over low heat. Add peanut butter, sugar, and vanilla. Mix well (batter will be very, very stiff). Spread in a 9½ × 6½-inch pan. Do not refrigerate.

Hint: Recipe can be varied with peanut butter morsels or butterscotch chips instead of chocolate. Also, you can substitute smooth peanut butter for the chunky and add your favorite nuts.

William J. Lambert, Jr.
Lincoln, Nebraska
Campin Sams

Bill's peanut brittle is microwave-easy. Serve for TV watching or for a snack on the road.

Serves 10

Microwave Peanutty Brittle

1½ cups unsalted or raw peanuts, or unsalted mixed nuts
1 cup sugar
½ cup white corn syrup
1 teaspoon vanilla
2 tablespoons margarine or butter
2 teaspoons baking soda

In a microwave-proof 2-quart glass measuring cup, mix nuts, sugar, and corn syrup. Microwave on high for 4 minutes. Remove and stir with wooden spoon. Cook an additional 4 minutes on high. Remove from oven and add vanilla and margarine or butter and stir. Cook for 2 minutes on high. Remove from oven and stir in baking soda. Spread on greased 10 × 15-inch cookie sheet and allow to cool and set. When hard, break into small pieces.

Robert L. Jairell
Laramie, Wyoming
Gem City Sams

This tasty treat takes only minutes to prepare and can be served as a TV snack. The ability to use substitutes makes this an especially flexible recipe, taking advantage of ingredients on hand.

Serves 4 to 6

Caramel Corn Supreme

1 cup unpopped popcorn, or microwave popcorn
2 cups (4 sticks) butter or margarine
2 cups granulated sugar *or* brown sugar
½ cup white corn syrup *or* pancake syrup
2 cups nuts (walnuts, pecans, or other)

Pop corn in popcorn popper, heavy pan, or microwave oven following directions on label. Set aside.

Bring butter, sugar, and syrup to boil; reduce heat and cook for 10 minutes, stirring constantly. Pour mixture over popped corn. Stir in nuts until popcorn and nuts are well coated. Stir while cooling or separate mixture on waxed paper.

Staff Recipes

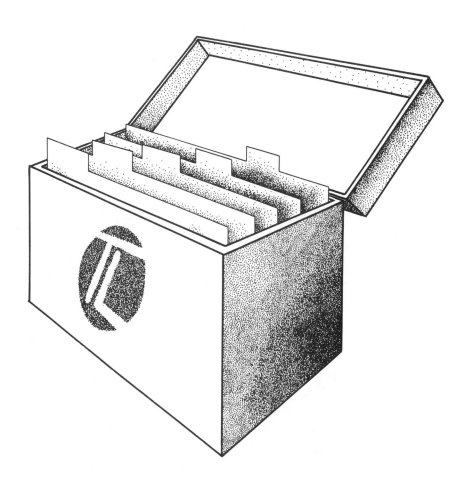

Hazel Van Osdol
International Sambassador
Hutchinson, Kansas

Hazel is the one who does the cooking when the Van Osdols are on the road as International Sambassadors for the Good Sam Club, but Steamboat does his share of the eating. Hazel likes this casserole because it is quick and simple to prepare, and it's one of Steamboat's favorites.

Serves 2

Steamboat's Tuna Casserole

1 package macaroni and cheese dinner
1 cup drained peas
1 10¾-ounce can cream of mushroom soup
1 7-ounce can tuna
½ cup cracker crumbs or potato chips

Preheat oven to 350°F. Prepare macaroni and cheese dinner following directions on package. Mix in peas, soup, and tuna. Pour into casserole dish and top with crumbs. Bake for 20 to 25 minutes.

A Sad Recipe

I didn't have potatoes, so I substituted rice.
I didn't have paprika, so I used another
    spice.
I didn't have tomato sauce, so I used tomato
    paste.
A whole can, not a half can; I don't believe
    in waste.
A friend gave me this recipe,
She said you couldn't beat it.
There must be something wrong with her,
    I couldn't even eat it!

Anonymous, submitted by Marian Hatch, Torrance, California, Member at Large

Martha T. McCarty
Editor
RV Buyers Guide

This scrumptious dip is gobbled up quickly whenever Martha makes it. It is wonderful with crackers and crunchy thin bread slices, and even better with crisp raw vegetables. It also makes an unusual and delicious topping for baked potatoes.

Makes 1 quart

Spinach Dip

| 2 cups sour cream |
| 1 cup mayonnaise |
| 1 3.5-ounce package leek soup mix (Martha uses Knorr's) |
| 1 10-ounce package frozen spinach, thawed, drained, and chopped twice |
| ½ cup chopped green onion |
| 1 teaspoon salad seasoning mix |
| 1 teaspoon dill |
| Pinch garlic powder |

Combine all ingredients well. Refrigerate for at least 24 hours before serving to allow flavors to combine.

Hint: *Look in the gourmet or imported food section of the grocery store if you can't find the leek soup mix in the soup section.*

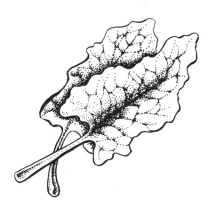

Life is too short to stuff a mushroom.

Shirley Conran, *Superwoman,* 1978

Marion Warren
Systems Manager
Typesetting

Wondering what he could do with some chicken pieces Marion had left out to defrost, Barrie, her husband, concocted this great oven-to-table, one-dish meal and surprised not only his wife and son, but himself as well.

Serves 3 to 4

Chicken Cacciatore

4 chicken breasts, skinned and halved
2 medium potatoes, sliced
1 carrot, sliced
1 medium onion, sliced
1 cup frozen peas
1 cup frozen mixed vegetables (any kind)
1 cup prepared spaghetti sauce

Place chicken in microwave-safe casserole. Layer all the vegetables on and around the chicken. Pour the spaghetti sauce over the top. Cover and microwave on high for 45 minutes, rotating the dish every 10 minutes.

Flo Cooper
Benecia, California
International Sambassador

As International Sambassadors, Ken and Flo attend a lot of Samborees and camp-outs where they like to entertain. This is one of Flo's party treats that always gets rave reviews.

Serves 6 to 8

Dessert Crisps With Apricot Sauce

Chips
Vegetable oil to cover bottom of skillet to 1½ inches
12 flour tortillas
⅓ cup confectioners sugar
Sauce
1 12-ounce jar apricot jam
1 to 2 teaspoons Grand Marnier or orange juice

For chips: Heat oil over high heat. Cut tortillas into wedges. Deep fry until crisp. Drain well. Sprinkle with confectioners sugar. **For dip:** Thin jam with liqueur or juice. Arrange chips on platter around dipping sauce in small bowl.

Hint: For variety, use different flavored jam and liqueur.

Judi Lazarus
Managing Editor
RV Buyers Guide

Judi's versatile fruit compote can accompany roast beef or poultry, or serve as a dessert with whipped topping. It's convenient for RVers because the ingredients can be varied according to taste and availability. It's delicious with fresh fruit, too.

Serves 20

"Delicious"

1 12-ounce package crispy macaroons
1 29-ounce can pear halves
1 29-ounce can sliced peaches
1 16-ounce can apricot halves
1 20-ounce can pineapple chunks
1 12-ounce package pitted prunes
Liqueur to taste (optional)

Preheat oven to 350°F. Crumble macaroons into medium-size pieces. Drain juices from canned fruit, reserving about ¼. Pour fruit juice into a 2-quart casserole to about 1-inch depth. Sprinkle a layer of macaroons over bottom of casserole. Mix fruits together in bowl, and spoon a layer of fruit over macaroons. Add another layer of macaroons and a small amount of liqueur and/or juice to casserole. Continue layers, finishing with macaroons on top. Pour remaining juice or liqueur over top and bake, covered, 30 minutes. Remove cover and bake 15 minutes longer. Can be served hot or cold.

Hint: If using fresh fruit, allow a little more liquid (use any fruit juice) and a little more baking time. Proportions can be varied; experiment with flavors you like.

Elizabeth Folk
Montgomery, Pennsylvania
International Sambassador

*Although Elizabeth and Emory
cover the continent from Canada to
Mexico as International
Sambassadors, they like their back-
home cooking. This chowder is one of
their favorite lunches.*

Serves 4

Elizabeth's Clam Chowder

1 10¾-ounce can New England-style clam chowder
1 10¾-ounce can cream of celery soup
1 6½-ounce can chopped clams
2 soup cans milk
6 eggs, hard-boiled and chopped
Black pepper (optional)

In medium pan, combine soups, clams, and milk. Bring to boil and remove from heat. Add eggs and pepper. Serve hot.

Hint: If you want thicker soup, use less milk or add a small amount of instant potato flakes.

Sue Bray
Executive Director
Good Sam Club

*When Sue was a little girl in her
native New Zealand, a visit to her
grandmother's house meant being
treated to a big serving of
Grandma's Trifle. Today, Sue
is the one making trifle for her
own two children.*

Serves 16

Grandma's Trifle

1 5⅛-ounce package vanilla pudding mix
1 large pound cake, sliced (homemade or purchased)
1 14-ounce jar raspberry jam
¼ to ½ cup port wine
2 cups whipping cream, whipped
Fresh fruit in season (Sue prefers kiwi fruit and sliced strawberries or bananas)

Prepare pudding according to directions on package. In large, flat-bottomed bowl or baking dish, place ½ of the pound cake slices. Spread on ½ of the raspberry jam. Lace with wine. Spread on ½ of the whipped cream. Repeat layers. Chill. Before serving, arrange sliced fruit over top.

Lawrence Lake
Free-lance Artist

When fresh corn is in season, Lawrence dons his chef's hat and prepares his favorite outdoor dinner. Serve it on paper plates and give the cleanup crew the night off.

Serves 4 to 6

Hobo Dinner

8 to 10 ears corn on the cob
12 small red potatoes, approximately
1½ to 2 pounds Italian or Polish sausage
1 cup (2 sticks) butter or margarine, melted
1 pint half and half
Salt and pepper to taste

Arrange cleaned corn around perimeter of 1-gallon potato chip can with ears standing on end. Fill middle with potatoes. Coil sausage over potatoes and corn. Add remaining ingredients. Cover can; punch hole in top. Place can over coals until steam emits from hole in top of can. Steam for 20 minutes. Remove meat and vegetables with tongs.

Hint: Reserve cooking liquid to pour over the corn. This meal can be prepared and frozen until time for your barbecue.

I eat my peas with honey
I've done it all my life.
It makes the peas taste funny,
But it keeps them on the knife.

Anonymous, Manners

Rena Copperman
General Manager
Book Division

Rena's grandmother used to make these wonderful, flaky, filled cookies. She has since duplicated the recipe and thinks that they are every bit as good as she remembers.

Makes 24

Rifka Rachel's Hungarian Kifle

Dough

2 cups sifted flour

1 cake compressed yeast

½ cup (1 stick) margarine

2 egg yolks

½ cup sour cream

Confectioners sugar

Melted margarine

Filling

1 cup finely chopped walnuts

½ cup sugar

1 teaspoon vanilla

2 egg whites, stiffly beaten

For dough: Put sifted flour in a large mixing bowl. Crumble in compressed yeast. Cut in margarine with pastry blender until mixture is crumbly.

Add egg yolks and sour cream; mix well. Form into a ball. On lightly floured board, knead until smooth, about 5 to 10 minutes. Divide dough into 3 equal parts. Wrap in waxed paper and chill in refrigerator at least 1 hour.

On a board sprinkled with confectioners sugar, roll each part of the dough into an 8-inch circle. Cut each circle into 8 pie-shaped wedges.

For filling: Combine walnuts, sugar, and vanilla. Fold in stiffly beaten egg whites.

For cookies: Preheat oven to 375°F. Fill wide end of each wedge with 1 tablespoon filling. Roll up from wide end to point. Place on greased baking sheet, curving ends to form crescent shape.

Bake 25 minutes, or until golden brown. Dust with confectioners sugar. Store in airtight container or freeze for later use.

Irma Ellison
Boerne, Texas
International Sambassador

Irma acquired this recipe from her grandmother who was from Alabama. Husband Bob is first in line at a camp-out potluck when he sees Irma preparing his favorite dessert.

Serves 24

Irma's Apple Slices

2½ cups flour
1 cup plus 2 tablespoons sugar
1 teaspoon salt
1 cup lard
1 egg yolk, combined with enough milk to make ⅔ cup
1½ cups cornflakes
8 to 10 medium apples, peeled and thinly sliced
1 teaspoon cinnamon
1 egg white
1 cup confectioners sugar, mixed with just enough water or milk to make thin glaze

Preheat oven to 400°F.

Combine flour, 2 tablespoons sugar, salt, and lard. Add egg yolk-milk mixture to dough and mix. Divide dough in half and roll out one portion. Line either a 9 × 13 × 2-inch baking pan or jelly roll pan. Sprinkle with cornflakes. Arrange sliced apples over cornflakes.

Combine 1 cup sugar and cinnamon; sprinkle over apples. Roll out remaining dough for top crust. Cover apples and crimp edges firmly. Beat egg white and brush over crust. Bake 1 hour. While still hot, drizzle with glaze made from confectioners sugar and water.

Martha McCarty
Editor
RV Buyers Guide

Janie Reyes grew up on a rancho in Guanajuato, Mexico. Each weekend she and her mother would make tortillas. By the end of the week, when the tortillas had become stale, they would use them in this recipe. With bacon and a green salad, it makes a great dinner at the end of a long day's drive. All of the ingredients are easily stored in Martha's little RV refrigerator.

Serves 4

Janie's Eggs and Tortillas

| 2 tablespoons margarine or butter |
| 1 small onion, chopped |
| ½ green pepper, diced (optional) |
| 2 corn tortillas, torn into 8 pieces each |
| 4 large eggs |
| 2 tablespoons milk |
| Salsa (¼ cup for recipe and additional to be added at table) |
| 1 cup grated cheese (Martha prefers cheddar or Jack) |

In medium-large skillet, melt butter or margarine. Add onion and green pepper, and sauté until softened. Add tortilla pieces and stir constantly until tortillas are soft—be careful not to let them become crisp.

Beat eggs with milk; add to pan and scramble until eggs are softly set. Add salsa and continue to scramble. Just before eggs set, remove from heat. Sprinkle mixture with grated cheese. Serve.

Give the guest food to eat even though you yourself are starving.

Anonymous, Arab saying

Bob Tinnon
Free-lance Designer

Bob's different salad is perfect for busy RVers—just mix and chill.

Serves 6 to 8

Fiesta Salad

1 cup mayonnaise
1 tablespoon chili powder
1 teaspoon catsup or chili sauce
Dash of cayenne pepper
Salt and pepper to taste
1 16-ounce can kidney beans
1 cucumber, diced
1 small onion, finely chopped
1 green pepper, diced
3 large tomatoes, diced
4 slices bacon, cooked and crumbled

Combine mayonnaise and seasonings in large bowl. Drain beans and other vegetables. Mix all ingredients together except for bacon, and chill. Add bacon just before serving.

To be miserly towards your friends is not pretty. To be miserly towards yourself is contemptible.

Norman Douglas, *Venus in the Kitchen*, 1952

Steve Troulman
Business Manager

Steve's avocado dip will liven up your happy hour. It can be mild or spicy, depending on the salsa used for seasoning.

Steve's Guacamole

4 ripe avocados, peeled, pitted, and mashed
½ large tomato, finely chopped
1 green onion, finely chopped
Chopped cilantro to taste
1 tablespoon mayonnaise
Salsa to taste

Combine avocado, tomato, onion, and cilantro. Add mayonnaise and mix thoroughly. Add salsa to taste and serve with taco or tortilla chips.

Thou sparkling bowl! thou sparkling bowl!
Though lips of bards thy rim may press . . .
I will not touch thee; for there clings
A scorpion to thy side, that stings!

John Pierpont, *The Sparkling Bowl*

Maxye S. Henry
Editorial Assistant
RV Business

Maxye named this recipe for the RV hosts who promise a seafood dinner, but haven't caught any. It's a delicate chowder—not too thick, and very colorful with the pink of the seafood and the yellow corn and green garnish.

Serves 4 to 6

Liar's Seafood Chowder

2 slices bacon, diced
1 clove garlic, minced
2 cups diced potatoes (about 4 medium)
1 cup dry white wine (Maxye prefers Chablis)
1 teaspoon celery salt
½ teaspoon thyme
⅛ teaspoon white pepper
1 6-ounce can shrimp, liquid reserved
1 6-ounce can crabmeat, liquid reserved
2 6½-ounce cans minced clams
1 17-ounce can cream-style corn
2 cups milk or half and half
Sliced green onions and parsley for granish

In a 3-quart saucepan, cook bacon and garlic until bacon is barely crisp.

Add potatoes, wine, seasonings, and seafood liquids. Simmer 15 to 20 minutes, until potatoes are tender. Add seafood, corn, and milk; heat thoroughly, but do not allow to boil. Garnish, and serve immediately.

Sherry McBride
Senior Editor
Trailer Life and MotorHome

This moist, delicious cake can be kept in the refrigerator for nearly a week, but Sherry says it never lasts that long! The ingredients are almost always available in your RV galley and the apples can be whatever kind you like. It's easy to whip up on the road because you only need 1 bowl, 1 saucepan, and 1 baking pan, and you don't really need to use an electric mixer.

Serves 9

Raw Apple Cake

Cake
1 egg
1 cup sugar
½ cup (1 stick) margarine or butter
1 cup sifted flour
¼ teaspoon salt
1 teaspoon nutmeg
1 teaspoon baking soda
2 cups coarsely grated apples (approximately 4)
Topping
¼ cup evaporated milk
¼ cup sugar
¼ cup (½ stick) margarine or butter
1 teaspoon vanilla

For cake: Preheat oven to 350°F. Cream together egg, sugar, and margarine or butter until light and fluffy.

Sift together flour, salt, nutmeg, and soda. Add to first mixture and stir until well blended. Stir in grated apples. Pour into 8 × 8 × 2-inch pan and bake 35 to 45 minutes.

For topping: While cake is baking, combine milk, sugar, and margarine or butter in 1-quart saucepan. Cook over medium heat 5 minutes; add vanilla.

When cake is done, pour topping over cake in pan. Allow to cool and cut into three rows in each direction.

When men reach their sixties and retire they go right to pieces. Women just go right on cooking.

Gail Sheehy

Judi Lazarus
Manager Editor
RV Buyers Guide

This salad is versatile because you can add chicken pieces or other protein to make it a main dish. The dressing is also a delicious addition to fresh fruit.

Serves 6 to 10

Special Spinach Salad

¼ cup vinegar
2 tablespoons water
1 1⅛-ounce package dry Italian dressing mix
3 tablespoons light brown sugar
2 tablespoons French-style mustard
Juice of 1 lemon
⅔ cup safflower oil (or any light vegetable oil)
2 bunches fresh spinach, washed and torn into bite-size pieces
1 cup fresh bean sprouts
1 tablespoon sesame seeds, toasted

Into 1-quart jar, add vinegar, water, and dressing mix; shake well. Stir in sugar, mustard, lemon juice, and oil. Shake well again. Let dressing sit awhile to allow flavors to combine.

Place spinach in bowl. Sprinkle with sprouts and sesame seeds. Shake dressing again and pour on a little at a time, tossing to coat each spinach leaf. Serve.

Spinach is the broom of the stomach.

Anonymous, French proverb

LaVonne Taylor-Pickell
Free-lance Editor

Most people don't enjoy okra, according to LaVonne, because they haven't had it properly prepared. Here is a golden opportunity to enjoy this different vegetable the way they do in Texas.

Serves 3 to 4

Texas Okra

1 pound okra, washed, trimmed, and cut in ⅛-inch-round slices
½ cup yellow cornmeal
½ teaspoon seasoned salt
¼ cup vegetable oil

Mix cornmeal and salt together. Put okra into a colander and pass under running water to dampen. Shake colander gently. Place okra into a plastic bag with cornmeal mixture and shake well to coat. Dry colander and put okra back into it, shaking gently to remove loose cornmeal.

Heat oil in frying pan. Add okra, stirring frequently, until golden brown. Serve immediately.

Angela Pezzullo
Typesetter

This Italian recipe is simple to make and will be a hit at your next get-together. It is delicious served hot with a salad, Italian bread, and a bottle of Chianti. It can also be served as an appetizer or an hors d'oeuvre.

Serves 6 to 8

Artichoke Pie

1 package frozen artichoke hearts, partly thawed and sliced
4 eggs, beaten
1 cup mozzarella cheese, shredded
½ cup pepperoni, diced
¼ cup Parmesan cheese, grated
1 teaspoon salt
½ teaspoon pepper
1 pie shell, partly baked

Preheat oven on 350°F.

Mix ingredients and pour into baked pie shell. Bake 45 minutes or until golden brown.

Julie Ann C. Vergel de Dios
Word Processing Coordinator

Julie says, "One of my rainy days was spent in the kitchen trying to make something new. I just got this recipe down pat when my husband, who was born in the Philippines, came home. When he saw what I was making he asked who taught me how to cook this well-known Filipino dish. So much for my creativity."

Serves 2 to 3

Lumpia Shanghai

1 12-ounce can roast beef with gravy (Julie prefers Hereford's Roast Beef)
1 19-ounce package eggroll wrappers
3 to 4 cups cooked rice
1 cup water
Enough oil to fry eggrolls

Drain gravy from roast beef and reserve. Shred beef into skillet. Heat over medium flame. Pour gravy into small mixing bowl and add water. Use whip or mixer to blend. Set aside.

Separate eggroll wrappers. (Be careful handling wrappers. They tear very easily if they are dry. You may have to use water to soften them.) Spread some water on counter and lay wrapper in water. Flip wrapper to wet both sides.

Add a small amount of meat and rice. Be careful not to overfill wrappers or they will not hold together when fried. Fold wrapper as you would a burrito.

Put into hot oil and cook both sides until golden brown. Make lumpia one at a time and fry immediately. If they sit too long they will become soggy. While lumpia is cooking, heat gravy in microwave or on stove and serve with Lumpia Shanghai as a sauce for dipping.

Hint: Don't be afraid to substitute pork, shrimp, or chicken. You may even want to add fresh vegetables. Take note that Lumpia Shanghai made without meat and containing vegetables is known simply as Lumpia.

Gale Urtel
Systems Book Manager
Typesetting

This dish was created for a party, and was such a success that Gale now prepares it often for her family dinners.

Serves 16

Pot Roast Mexicali

1 4-pound pot roast, chuck roast, or O-roast
1 cup Burgundy
1 1.5-ounce package onion soup mix
1 15-ounce can ranch style beans
1 15-ounce can kidney beans, drained
1 15-ounce can garbanzo beans, drained
1 15-ounce can pinto beans, drained
1 30-ounce can tamales, cut into cubes
1 10-ounce can enchilada sauce
1 10-ounce jar green chili salsa
Cheddar cheese, grated

Place roast in Dutch oven. Pour wine over meat and sprinkle with onion soup mix. Cover and cook 3 to 4 hours, or until meat is tender enough to shred.

Shred meat, reserving cooking liquid. In a large casserole dish add shredded meat, beans, tamales, sauces, and cooking liquid and mix well. Heat through and then refrigerate overnight.

When ready to bake, preheat oven to 350°F. Skim off fat, then bake 45 minutes.

Sprinkle generously with shredded cheese and bake another 15 minutes or until cheese has melted.

Hint: Serve with green salad and warm corn tortillas. Also good as filling for burritos.

Beef is the soul of cooking.

Antonin Carème, *Le Cuisinier Parisien*, 1828

Gale Urtel
Systems Book Manager
Typesetting

Gale's mousse has become famous at TL and is invariably served at staff parties.

Serves 20 to 30

Salmon Mousse

1 large can red salmon, liquid reserved
½ cup finely chopped celery
¼ cup finely chopped onion
2 ¼-ounce packages unflavored gelatin
½ cup cold water
¼ cup tarragon vinegar
¼ cup catsup
1 cup mayonnaise

Place salmon liquid in a small saucepan. Mix salmon, celery, and onion together. Mix gelatin in cold water to soften. Mix tarragon vinegar and catsup into salmon liquid and bring to boil. Add gelatin and boiled mixture to salmon and mix well. Add mayonnaise and mix again. Pour into oiled 6-cup mold. Chill to set. Serve with crackers or party bread.

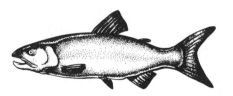

Seven make a banquet, nine make a noise.

Anonymous, Latin proverb 25

LaVonne Taylor-Pickell
Free-lance Editor

This old family recipe, handed down from generation to generation, originated before today's health-conscious cooking. But when LaVonne feels homesick, she cooks up a big batch and says, "Hang the cholesterol and calories!"

Serves 3 to 4

Texas Fried Steak

Steak
1 large round steak, tenderized and cut in serving-size pieces
½ cup white flour
1 teaspoon salt
1 teaspoon pepper
2 eggs, well beaten
Oil for cooking

Gravy
1 tablespoon flour
1 teaspoon granulated beef bouillon
1 cup water or milk

For steak: Preheat oven to 200°F. Mix flour with salt and pepper. Coat each piece of meat with egg, and then dredge both sides in flour mixture. Heat ¼ inch oil in large, heavy frying pan. When oil is hot, gently place each piece of meat into pan, being careful not to crowd pieces. Cook until well browned on each side. Put meat into oven to keep warm while you prepare gravy.

For gravy: Pour excess oil from pan, leaving about 1 tablespoon. Over low heat, add flour and brown well. Dissolve bouillon in water or milk. Remove pan from heat, and gradually pour bouillon mixture into pan, stirring briskly and continuously. Scrape the pan well while stirring to loosen meat particles. Pour gravy into boat and serve with meat.

Hint: Mashed potatoes or biscuits are the true Texas complements, according to LaVonne. Her father loved it with baby black-eyed peas and hot peppers.

Index

My Favorite Recipes

My Favorite Recipes

My Favorite Recipes

_____

_____

_____

_____

_____

_____

_____

_____

_____

_____

_____

_____

_____

_____

_____

_____

_____

_____

_____

_____

My Favorite Recipes

_____

_____

_____

_____

_____

_____

_____

_____

_____

_____

_____

_____

_____

_____

_____

_____

_____